PREPARING COUPLES *for* LOVE AND MARRIAGE

a pastor's resource

Cameron Lee and James L. Furrow

Abingdon Press™

Nashville

PREPARING COUPLES FOR LOVE AND MARRIAGE:
A PASTOR'S RESOURCE

Copyright © 2013 by Abingdon Press

All rights reserved.

This book is printed on acid-free paper.

Library of Congress Cataloging-in-Publication Data

Lee, Cameron.
  Preparing couples for love and marriage : a pastor's resource / by Cameron Lee and James L. Furrow.
      pages cm
  Includes bibliographical references.
  ISBN 978-1-4267-5320-6 (alk. paper)
  1. Marriage counseling. 2. Pastoral counseling. 3. Marriage—Religious aspects—Christianity. I. Title.
  BV4012.27.L44 2013
  259'.13—dc23
                                                                                                2013028244

Disclaimer: All names and significant details have been changed by the author to protect the identity of clients.

13 14 15 16 17 18 19 20 21 22—10 9 8 7 6 5 4 3 2 1

MANUFACTURED IN THE UNITED STATES OF AMERICA

Contents

Contents

Introduction

Couples invest a great deal of time, money, and energy in planning and enjoying their wedding ceremony—typically <u>much more than the effort expended on preparing for the marriage itself</u>. Pastors, for their part, find themselves in a unique role with couples anticipating marriage. Their approaches to preparing couples depend on training and interest. Some pastors are actually trained in counseling and the use of premarital inventories. Others simply recommend a book or a sermon series, often leaving the couple better prepared for their wedding than for the marriage that comes after. Certainly, careful wedding planning is necessary (we all have stories of wedding mishaps, don't we?), and there are many good books and sermons on marriage. We've often heard from couples, though, that their experiences at the more informal end of the spectrum weren't that helpful in preparing them for their postwedding reality. And we suspect that many pastors would do more if they had clearer direction or felt more confident that they knew what to do when meeting with the couple.

We've written this book to help provide that direction.

Here's part of the bigger picture. When it comes to marriage and divorce in America, there's both good news and bad news. First, the good news: according to the U.S. Census Bureau, the overall divorce rate is down. A half century ago, divorces skyrocketed, and reached their peak in the early 1980s. But since then, the divorce rate has been gradually tailing off.

The bad news? The divorce rate may be down, but it's not low, and those who stay married aren't necessarily happy. For example, using data from more than fifty thousand couples, family scholar David Olson reported that just under half of the couples studied could be classified as "unhappily married."[1]

And while the divorce rate is down, so is the marriage rate. Those who do marry are waiting longer to tie the knot, and meanwhile, the cohabitation rate continues its steep climb. Indeed, many couples believe that living together is a good way to find out if they can make a go of marriage—even though there's evidence that this is a deeply flawed strategy.[2] After all, <u>living together with the idea that the relationship can be dissolved when the going gets rough is a poor way to prepare for the vow of staying committed "for better or worse"</u>!

Thus, adults today often question if they have what it takes to make marriage work. Perhaps this is why more and more engaged couples are taking advantage of

[handwritten margin note: Stat: 50% of couples are unhappily married]

v

Strong marriages come from skills that are learned!

some form of premarital preparation.[3] Some couples read self-help books or go to workshops. Others attend counseling sessions that center on their responses to a premarital inventory (the PREPARE and the FOCCUS are two of the best known examples) that helps them identify important areas of difference.[4]

No one, of course, can guarantee relationship success, not even the most highly experienced and trained counselor. But we firmly believe in the value of proactively teaching engaged couples the skills they need to help keep their marriages strong and resilient. Neither the skills nor the teaching need to be complicated. Time and again, in marriage workshops, we've seen couples react in astonishment when they've finally resolved an issue that has stymied them for years—all because they were coached through a simple communication exercise that lasted *five minutes*.

Don't get us wrong. We're not saying that all marital problems can be solved in five minutes! But many marital arguments started as small problems that could have been worked out before they grew into bigger ones. Simply put, they began as *mismanaged interaction*. A husband, for example, may say something to upset his wife, often without meaning to. She snaps at him in anger, and he overreacts to her response. On it goes, through a familiar cycle of blame and hurt feelings that may be repeated again and again over the years. Spouses grow acutely sensitive to particular emotional slights, and negative patterns become nearly automatic.

Problems and conflicts will eventually visit every marriage. But what if couples had been taught to anticipate and stay out of those patterns to begin with? What if they entered marriage with the attitudes, beliefs, and skills they needed to manage their interactions more positively? What if they knew better how to turn the differences between them into strengths?

Therein lies the hope that drives the work of preparing couples for successful marriage. No one can smooth away all the rough spots in the marital road ahead. But couples can be taught to pay attention to warning signs, to know where the bumps or potholes are most likely to be, and to deal more skillfully with the hazards they encounter. Good preparation enables couples to take a first step together in facing their future challenges.

Our goal is to provide pastors with a basic framework and the tools to begin this ministry. You don't need any formal background in counseling, because the kind of work we're talking about isn't counseling—think of it as a series of *coached conversations* in which you help couples respond positively to the differences between them. It's not about having the answers to all their questions. It's about helping couples understand how they are different from each other and helping them learn the ideas and skills they need to accept and manage those differences long before they become a serious threat to the marriage.

The book is organized into three parts. The first part will orient you to the ministry of premarital preparation. Chapter 1 focuses on the basics. What is this kind of work about? What skills do *you* need? To prepare couples to succeed in marriage, you must model what you teach: pay attention not just to words but also to the relationship process; listen with full attention; speak in ways that build relationship. We will

"Pre-marital Conversations" or "Coached Conversations"

also address the topic of what to do when you suspect that the marriage is ill advised, and when to refer the couple to another professional.

Chapter 2 addresses the central dynamic around which your pastoral conversations will revolve—the personal differences that the bride and groom bring into their relationship. To illustrate, we'll deal with two of the most fundamental areas of difference: gender and culture. Men and women often approach relationships differently, and this is further complicated by the individuals' cultural and family backgrounds. This necessarily brief discussion will help set the tone for conversations about other areas of difference.

In chapter 3, we'll walk you through a flexible four-session process for using the *Conversation Jumpstarter,* a tool we've developed to organize the discussions you will be having with the couple. The Jumpstarter is a reproducible resource that the couple completes before the first session. It asks them to reflect on how things were done in several key areas in their families, and what related expectations they bring to the marriage. Each topic covered by the Jumpstarter is the subject of a later chapter in the book that will provide you with information and tips to help you coach conversations in each area.

Chapter 3 provides a detailed suggested plan for using the Jumpstarter in a flexible format that involves a preliminary meeting with the couple, followed by four full teaching or coaching sessions. If you're already comfortable working with couples, you may simply want to integrate the Jumpstarter and the other tools provided in this book into what you already do. We created these tools for pastors, but they could be assets to anyone coaching premarital couples, from counseling professionals to mentor couples volunteering in a congregation's marriage ministry.

Part 2 of the book will help you coach couples in the skills they need in order to deal with their differences constructively. Engaged couples already have a tendency to minimize these differences, preferring to emphasize the more ideal aspects of the relationship. Even those with a more sober eye can't anticipate all potential conflicts in advance. Most of us don't even know all the values and expectations we hold. We often don't become aware of them until they really matter or have been violated, and then we may feel upset without knowing why. And as we will suggest later, even the most successful of couples won't resolve all their differences.

But it's important for couples to learn a *process* for handling differences, whatever the *content* of the issue that threatens to divide them. Guiding couples through the process we describe will help instill in them a greater confidence in their relationship and in their ability to face important issues together.

Thus, in chapters 4 and 5, we'll describe the communication and relationship skills that you will help couples learn and practice, and in chapter 6, we'll focus on the skills and principles of coaching itself. In essence, your job is to create a safe and comfortable atmosphere for partners to share their stories, feelings, and opinions with each other while practicing skillful communication. In the appendices, we'll provide you with the handouts you need to guide the process, including the homework assignments they'll need to complete between sessions.

The chapters in part 3 follow the topics raised in the Jumpstarter. Differences of expectations in each of the following areas are common sources of conflict in marriage: roles, responsibilities, and the division of household labor (chapter 7); love and affection (chapter 8); money (chapter 9); decisions related to having and raising children (chapter 10); relationships with in-laws and extended family (chapter 11); and spiritual and devotional practices and goals (chapter 12).

The treatment of each subject will necessarily be brief. Each chapter begins with information that will give you some perspective on the issue at hand; each chapter ends with suggestions of additional resources for your further enrichment and that of the couple. In between, we will give suggestions regarding issues that the couple's discussion of the Jumpstarter may raise. A concluding epilogue points the way forward by locating the work of premarital preparation in its larger context of ministry and mission.

Thus, this book will guide you through a practical and relationally focused approach to premarital preparation. Each conversation engages the couple in an opportunity to increase their awareness and strengthen their commitment through discussing key issues while practicing the skills that promote resilient relationships. The process provides a way for couples to bolster their hope and confidence as they begin the adventure of building a successful marriage.

We are grateful for the opportunity to contribute to this growing area of ministry. Thanks go first to Kathy Armistead and the team at Abingdon Press for the faithful vision that birthed this project. Special and heartfelt appreciation goes to Jack and Judy Balswick, who have been our mentors, colleagues, and friends for many years. Their love of life together with their commitment to Christ and to each other has been an ongoing inspiration to us and many others. We also want to thank other professionals whose depth of insight and practical wisdom have helped form our own ways of thinking and working, as well as our deepening desire to help couples make the most of marriage: George Doub, Terry Hargrave, Patty Howell, Susan Johnson, and Ralph Jones.

To pastors wanting to add depth and breadth to their work with premarital couples, we thank you for taking time out of your busy schedules to read this book; we pray that the Holy Spirit will encourage you through it. Finally, thank you to our students in the Marriage and Family program at Fuller Theological Seminary who contributed their feedback and suggestions: Courtney Chang, Kathryn Johnson, Justin Little, Eun Hyey Lok, Rich Painter, Kaye Schneider, Samantha Smith, Luke Wilkerson, and Katie Welch. You and the other students in the program—past, present, and future—are a constant source of inspiration to us, helping us to remember the greater mission of which we are all a part. We look forward to how God will continue to use you to his glory and the well-being of couples and families everywhere. It is to all of you that we dedicate this book.

Pasadena, California
December 2012

Part One

Getting Started

C h a p t e r
O n e

The Basic Skills

Here's a story from my (Cameron's) own experience, a scenario with which many of you will no doubt identify. I'll get an e-mail from our church secretary: "Please contact so-and-so; she [or he] wants to know if you're available to do her [or his] wedding." I don't recognize the name but dutifully return the call.

For a second or two, the person can't figure out who I am. Then the light goes on—*Oh, right, this is the guy the lady at that church told us about.* The voice at the other end brightens: "Thanks so much for calling back!" We exchange a few pleasantries, then she or he cuts to the chase: "We were wondering if you would be available to officiate at our wedding."

"Possibly," I reply. "When is it?"

"Next weekend."

Inwardly, I sigh, then politely decline, explaining that my policy is to require couples to go through a preparation process first, with me or someone else. The conversation usually ends very quickly after that.

I love weddings. I cherish the opportunity to speak into the lives of two people who desire to be joined in the God-given institution called marriage. So it troubles me to think that for some couples, the minister is almost an afterthought, a functionary whose main purpose is to sign the marriage license.

Surely we can do better, and our assumption is that you're reading this book because you would agree. You believe that marriage is too important to be entered lightly, and want to help couples understand what they're getting themselves into and be better prepared.

This book is intended as a short and practical guide to premarital preparation. To make this resource as broadly useful as possible, we don't assume that you will be working only with Christian couples, though that may be your choice. Rather, this book is written as a guide for helping both Christian *and* non-Christian couples get off to a good start in marriage.

3

Practically speaking, most of the premarital couples who come to you may do so because they need someone to officiate their wedding. You may know one or both of the partners directly, or they may be related to someone in your church, or they may be total strangers who picked your name out of a phone book. One, both, or neither may be Christians. And you will have to make your own policies about the conditions under which you will say yes.[1]

Because pastors vary greatly in those policies (and whether or not they have any), the process we describe in these pages may not look much like what you would normally consider to be "pastoral counseling." You may wish to teach couples a biblical view of marriage, but that won't be our focus here.[2] There may be opportunities to give spiritual guidance or to help them solve problems, but that's not the primary emphasis either. Rather, the task of premarital preparation, as envisaged in this book, is twofold. First, you will be creating a hospitable space for them to talk to each other about things that could become difficult after they're married. And second, you will be coaching them in the basic skills they need for those conversations to be constructive and relationship building.

Thus, we assume that you already have your own commitments about when and how to exercise the ministry of spiritual guidance that is intrinsic to your pastoral office. Here, we want to show you a way of working with premarital couples that we think of as a ministry of compassion, both to those who ask you to officiate and to those who may come to you because of a broader ministry you may have in order to strengthen marriage in your church and community.

Our general goal is to help you create a safe and positive climate for engaged couples to anticipate critical issues and to practice managing their differences in ways that strengthen rather than undermine their commitment to each other. By implication, this means that your primary task in working with these couples is *not* to identify and solve their problems. We repeat: *your job is not to help the couple fix their problems before they marry!*

Why? In the first place, even if it could be accomplished, it's far too daunting a task for the relatively few hours you will spend with them. But second, and more important, such a goal may fail to reflect what makes for a truly stable relationship in the real world. As marriage researcher John Gottman has argued, even in the most successful of marriages, only a fraction of relationship problems actually "get solved." Instead, the majority become what Gottman calls "perpetual issues."[3]

That may sound like throwing a big wet blanket over our hopes for marriage and for premarital preparation. But it pays to be realistic. All couples—even the most mature of Christian couples—have "perpetual issues." Some problems come up over and over and never get resolved. This is not, however, a counsel of despair. Gottman's point is that even though successful couples don't always resolve their differences, they handle these differences a way that reflects a positive and accepting relationship.

No marriage preparation process, no matter how worthy, is farsighted or thorough enough to remove all barriers to a successful relationship. So-called perpetual issues can't always be predicted in advance. Your more limited and realistic task is to

Pastoral Conversations —
→ It's not about resolving all differences, but learning to resolve differences

help couples learn to deal with their differences in a way that doesn't dissolve their unity. Essentially, you will be giving them a head start on married life by coaching them through a difficult conversation or two so that they will be better prepared to handle such conversations on their own.

That's why we avoid the term "premarital counseling" in this book. Many people go to counselors with the expectation that they will air and then solve their problems. Therefore, if you call it "counseling," couples will look to you—or literally, during a session, look *at* you—for answers. If you're comfortable being in that position, and have the training to help couples in that way, great. If not, don't create false expectations. Be consistent in calling this a ministry of marriage "preparation" in which you function as a coach rather than a counselor, and help couples understand the difference (we'll say much more about coaching in chapter 6).

Many of you, at some point, have had some training in communication skills, to help you be a better listener in the context of pastoral counseling. Use whatever skills and knowledge you already have in order to make the process work for you. In this book, however, we don't assume that you have any such formal training. Five fundamental skills will therefore be described briefly below, and some will be touched on again in later chapters. For now, read the descriptions and ask yourself, "Is this something I already do well? Do I need to be more intentional about learning or practicing this?"

Skill 1: Pay Attention to Process "How" over "what"

One of the most important distinctions to keep in mind when working with couples and their communication is *content* versus *process.* Learn to recognize the difference in your own interactions, and drill it into the couples you work with, every chance you get.

The basic idea is this: *what* people communicate or fight or argue about (the content) is usually not nearly as important as *how* they do it (the process). That's not to say that content doesn't matter. Some fights are about things that matter deeply, making it harder to stay calm. A disagreement about whether or not to have children, for example, will likely be more heated or anxiety provoking than one about where to go for dinner! But it's in the process—the *how* of communication—that the conversation goes off the rails.

Couples, and the people who try to help them, often focus too much on the content of an argument, as if sitting down and poring over a typed transcript of the interchange could resolve the problem. You've probably experienced this kind of argument yourself. "You said X." "I never said any such thing." "Ooh, I wish I had a recording—I'd prove it to you."

But even if one could magically produce such a recording, would it end the disagreement? Would someone really admit, "Hey, you're right; I *did* say that! I'm sorry; I don't know what I was thinking"? Not likely. In fact, couples can drag a fight out for ten or fifteen minutes and then completely forget how the argument started. By that time, it's not about the "issue" anymore. It's about winning, or simply defending one's point of view.

People don't just object to *what* their spouse says, but also *how* he or she says it. It's not just the words used, but also the nonverbal cues with which the words are packaged. People may react strongly, for example, to a hard or mocking edge in their spouse's tone of voice, or the way he or she rolls his or her eyes in contempt. If they were to notice and express what was going on inside of them, they might say things like: *It scares me when you raise your voice that way;* or, *When I see you standing there with your hands on your hips, I feel like a stupid little kid;* or, *When you don't respond back to me, I feel ignored and alone;* or, *I feel demeaned when you criticize what you think I've done wrong, without noticing what I've done right.*

Preparing couples for successful marriage includes helping them to avoid getting mired in an endless and unproductive battle of words. And that means that you, as their coach, also have to be careful not to get tangled in their verbal web. Don't just listen to the content of the words; listen for how the words are said, and watch how the other person responds. What do you hear in the tone of voice? What do you see in each person's face and body language?

For example, let's say a couple is telling you the story of how they met (which they will do in your first full meeting with them). They both agree that they saw a movie on their first date, but disagree on which movie it was. Who's right isn't really important—but how they handle the disagreement is. Pay attention to *how* they disagree. Do they argue playfully, with genuine affection? That's a good sign. Or does he roll his eyes at her and then turn to you and make a disparaging remark such as, "See what I have to put up with?"

Does one person do all the talking while the other sits quietly? That's not necessarily a problem in itself, but it tells you something about their relationship. Or do they both talk at once and overlap each other? If so, how does one respond to the interruptions of the other? Does it feel like two people working to build a story together, or competing to be the one who gets to tell it the "right" way?

Making neutral comments about what you see and hear in the process helps them to have more insight into their relationship. A simple observation, delivered matter-of-factly, will often suffice: "Jacob, I noticed that when Rachel started talking about how much she wanted kids, you sighed and looked down at the floor." You don't need to interpret or explain the behavior. Just help them notice and be more curious about each other's responses, and be prepared to direct the ensuing conversation.

Skill 2: Model Attentive Listening

Virtually every marriage enrichment curriculum teaches both listening and speaking skills. Although both sets of skills are closely intertwined, attentive and empathic listening is more foundational. Why? Even if everyone in the world were superbly gifted at speaking, it wouldn't make any difference if no one listened well.

But if everyone listened with full attention, wanting to understand, even the most awkward attempts at speaking could still result in connection.

To effectively teach couples to be humble and attentive listeners, you have to begin by serving as a living example. This is especially important for those who are in ministry. We make our living with the spoken word. People turn to us for answers and advice, or even the occasional scolding from the pulpit. These have their proper place. But when others don't follow our sage counsel, it's often because we've failed to listen and therefore have not truly understood either the person or the problem.

You'll find a thorough discussion of listening skills in chapter 4. For now, consider these guidelines:

Focus Your Attention on the Person Who Is Speaking

Busy and distracted people find good listening a challenge. They think they can listen with their ears while their eyes remain glued to the television. Their minds are preoccupied with their to-do lists, or with what they're going to say back to the other person in response.

Does that describe *you* as well? Good listening requires making mental space for other people and their words. Tuning into people means tuning out other things, which can mean actually turning your body toward them and away from distractions. Be curious about what they have to say. Focus on hearing and understanding their words. It's amazing what can happen when people feel they have your full attention.

Remember That It's Important to Listen Even When You Don't Agree

Again, an occupational hazard: as a pastor, you want to encourage people in their pursuit of holy living. That means that sometimes you feel it's your job to correct people. In a conversation, a couple may tell you something that triggers a silent alarm: "Wait—they're already sleeping together? Yikes! How do I fix this?" At that point, your own anxious thoughts may get in the way of listening, because you feel that your pastoral responsibilities require you to *do* something.

We're not asking you to abandon your role as a spiritual guide. But remember that your ability to speak into a couple's life depends on their being able to listen to what you say. And that won't happen unless they feel heard by you, which brings us to the next point.

The Goal Is for the Other Person to Feel Heard and Understood

Learning listening skills is not an end in itself, as if mechanically following a particular set of guidelines were all that mattered. Successful relationships are built on empathy and trust, and these in turn are fostered where people *feel* heard. You must model attentive listening in your sessions if you want to motivate couples to create the same respectful climate in their marriages.

Skill 3: Get Comfortable with Silence

There may be people in your life with whom you can sit quietly without having the need to fill in the silence with words. Hopefully, God falls in that category, as well as your spouse and children, if any. But at times, a lull in a conversation can feel maddening. You worry about what the other person is thinking or feeling, or what, if anything, you should say!

Sometimes, a little clarifying communication could help. For example, a couple may not respond to a question you've asked, because they don't understand it. Again, pay attention to the nonverbal cues: do they seem lost or confused? If so, check in with them: "You seem puzzled. Did my question make sense?"

But often, your conversations will veer into uncomfortable and possibly uncharted territory, whether by accident or design. Deep emotions have been triggered, and people turn inward, uncertain how to respond. Watch their eyes. Are they looking down or away in shame? Or are they looking up in thoughtful consideration?

This is often a crucial juncture from which new insight may spring. Don't rush it. Avoid the temptation to jump in prematurely with words. Continue to focus with compassionate attention. Use the moment to pray silently for the sanctifying work of the Holy Spirit in their lives—and in yours. Release your own anxiety about the process to God, and be patient. Your patience is a sign of your care.

Skill 4: Stay on Task

If you have all the time in the world to work with the couple, and they're not paying you for your time, you may have more freedom for long, leisurely conversations. But where the time frame is limited or money is involved, you don't have that luxury.[4] It's your responsibility to structure your time together. That doesn't mean you have to be a rigid taskmaster! But neither should sessions be treated as if they were chance meetings over coffee. Depending on your personality, you may need to make a conscious effort to be more directive. Here are two guidelines to keep in mind.

Discuss the Structure and Your Expectations Up Front

Couples entering some kind of premarital preparation need to know what's involved. They may already have their own questions: How often will you meet? How long are the sessions? What will they be asked to do?

In this book, of course, we propose our own answers. In chapter 3, we'll introduce you to the Conversation Jumpstarter, a resource you can use to structure your time together and the couple's expectations, with room for flexibility as the need arises. But whether you use our tool or someone else's, the point is to make the structure clear before the preparation process begins. You can also reiterate the expectations at the beginning or end of each session: "Today [or next time], what we're going to do is . . ." Strategic reminders like this will keep the couple focused and help you stay on task together.

Interrupt and Redirect When Necessary

Some people simply enjoy the chance to talk and to have someone listen attentively. And you may have been taught that it's not polite to interrupt. When those two are put in combination, you can end up with an individual or couple who starts talking and hardly pauses for breath, while you're sneaking peeks at your watch and wondering when you'll be able to squeeze a word in edgewise.

Try to keep the conversation focused. In chapter 6, we'll describe in more detail how to jump in and redirect the process when necessary. For now, recognize that the ability to listen attentively and to be patient with silence must be balanced with the ability to keep couples on task. If you feel uncomfortable with the idea of interrupting people—even when you think you should—give particular attention to developing this skill.

Skill 5: Refer When Appropriate

Once they get to know you and feel comfortable with the process, some engaged couples will begin to show you the more troublesome aspects of their relationship. You'll have your suspicions about which couples will make it and which won't. Sometimes you'll be right—but not always. You probably already know couples who have built a stable, caring relationship on nothing but emotional scraps from their own backgrounds. Realistically, not only do successful couples have perpetual issues after they're married, they sometimes begin with what seem to be serious challenges.

We're not suggesting that you ignore such challenges—just be wary of overconfident predictions. Only rarely, if ever, would we actually advise telling a couple not to marry. And though you could politely decline to perform the wedding ceremony, you should only do this if (a) they knew this was a possibility in advance, and (b) you've begun the process early enough to give them time to find another minister.

What's the alternative? Begin with the principle of respect, as suggested by the Code of Ethics of the American Association for Marriage and Family Therapy (AAMFT): "Marriage and family therapists respect the rights of clients to make decisions and help them to understand the consequences of these decisions."[5] In other words, simply telling a couple, "I don't think you should get married," doesn't adequately respect the fact that the decision is both their right and their responsibility.

But you can still offer respectful counsel. Again, you can make an observation about the process, and open the door to alternatives: "This is a really important and difficult issue for both of you, and you obviously don't agree. I'm wondering if you need more time to sort this out before you get married." Or you can directly name the problem area while still leaving the decision to them: "If you decide to marry, you're probably going to keep struggling with this issue of whose career is going to determine where you live."

You can also recommend that they work more closely with a marital therapist, either immediately or after the wedding. If you're referring them because of their conversation around the Jumpstarter, recommend that they take their written responses with them to the first session, to help create some context. It's up to the counselor to decide whether or not to use the documents, but they could be a valuable resource in jumpstarting that conversation as well. Meanwhile, when do you refer, and to whom?

When Should You Refer?

There will be times when you are sitting with a couple and your "gut sense" is telling you that this couple needs more help than you can give. When this happens, trust your gut and recognize the limits of your time and training. Remember, our focus is marriage preparation, not couples counseling. Here are five warning signs that we believe signal that a couple would benefit from mental health treatment.

Rigid thinking. Sometimes, one partner dominates a discussion with an inflexible and polarized "all or nothing" position. His or her rigidity shuts down discussion. Pushing back against this inflexibility gets you more of the same, with added intensity. These defensive responses suggest that other underlying issues are at work and that the exercises in our program will probably be of limited benefit.

Reactive conflict. Couple conflicts often follow negative patterns of emotional experience that have an ongoing history in their relationship. Our marriage preparation exercises can trigger these conflicts; as the argument escalates, partners are no longer discussing differences but fighting about their relationship. Couples who consistently escalate in this way will benefit from the more structured setting of marital therapy, where strong emotions can be experienced and worked through more thoroughly.

Unfinished business. At times partners may bring up past experiences or family issues they continue to confront. At one level this should be expected because weddings tend to intensify family dynamics. Family histories may involve traumatic memories that influence a partner's ability to trust or be vulnerable. Although these are appropriate responses to past trauma, they can block intimacy in the present. Therapy can be an important resource to help individuals heal their hurtful pasts. Coaching the other partner to be supportive in this process encourages the couple to face these challenges together, while leaving room for each partner to face the past on his or her own terms.

Lingering ambivalence. Marriage is a significant step of commitment; a case of "cold feet" is not uncommon. Ongoing ambivalence about marriage in general or the relationship in particular, however, is an important signal. Planning a wedding creates its own momentum, so it's important to pay attention to partners who show consistent reluctance or uncertainty. Premarital preparation helps couples anticipate the issues they may face in marriage, but individual or couples therapy provides a better context for exploring this kind of ambivalence and its implication for each person's future.

Active abuse. Discussing a couple's relationship can bring issues of personal safety to the fore. The impact of abuse can be severe, despite the partners' best intentions, and safety is essential to establishing a meaningful basis of trust in marriage. Evidence of emotional, psychological, or physical abuse, therefore, will require a referral to a more intensive level of care. Similarly, the presence of substance abuse in a relationship may necessitate further evaluation and treatment. Couples may make light of the symptoms and behaviors associated with these problems, so your referral may be simply for the purpose of assessment when the evidence is unclear.

To Whom Should You Refer?

Not all therapy is created equal. Counseling couples and counseling individuals are two very different things, requiring different training. Bottom line: if you're going to refer a couple to therapy for relationship issues, you need to send them to someone who is trained to do this and has an established track record of success.

Ideally, you would refer to a professional whom you already know and trust—someone who shares your values and beliefs about the importance and sanctity of marriage, and who will support your pastoral role. If you don't know anyone who fits that bill, and you want to begin a ministry of coaching premarital couples, find someone as soon as possible.

Where do you begin? How a therapist is licensed is the first clue. People who are licensed as marital and family therapists have been specifically trained to work with couples. That's not to say that a licensed psychologist or even a psychiatrist would *not* have that training, but you would have to ask him or her to find out. You can find marital and family therapists online through resources like www.therapistlocator.net, a service provided by the AAMFT.

Be aware, though, that not every marriage therapist will have values that align with yours. In a "divorce culture" such as ours, even some marriage therapists lean more toward helping couples part amicably than toward helping them fight for the marriage.

How can you tell the difference? One resource is the National Registry of Marriage Friendly Therapists, a listing of professionals who subscribe to a "balanced pro-commitment stance."[6] Therapists listed in the registry believe in the value of healthy and lifelong marriage, and orient toward that goal whenever possible.

You're not just looking to outsource counseling; you're building a community-wide team. Try the resources above. Ask people in your congregation for the names of counselors they've worked with and would recommend to others. Once you've identified local therapists who could potentially serve as referrals, meet with them. Explain who you are and what you're doing; share your overall ministry goals. Ask questions: What is their training? How often do they actually work with couples? How many couples have they actually helped to put their marriage back together?

What relationship do they have to a church, if any? What kind of relationship would they envision having with you and your ministry? Building trust in your referrals will give you greater confidence in your work with couples because you have more resources to help couples in need.

In short, you'll need the five skills we've described to prepare couples for marriage, whatever procedure you use. The specific method we will teach you revolves around helping couples acknowledge and deal constructively with the differences between them, the importance of which is the topic of the next chapter.

Chapter Two

Dealing with Difference

Her family celebrates on Christmas Eve. It's a raucous party scene. The house is full of siblings, cousins, aunts, and uncles. People are shouting and laughing. Multiple presents are being handed out at once; some of them are gag gifts. No one waits for anyone else. Wrapping paper is being ripped with gleeful abandon, and ribbons are being tossed on the floor.

His family celebrates on Christmas Day. It's a small gathering. People sit quietly in a circle. Presents are handed out one at a time. Everyone watches politely as the recipient unwraps the gift, sometimes carefully peeling back the tape so as not to damage the expensive paper—which may get reused. The gift is held out for all to see, polite words are exchanged, and the ritual is repeated with the next person.

The two get married. Their respective families live near each other, so there's no negotiation needed as to where to go for the holidays—Christmas Eve is with her family, Christmas Day is with his. But the juxtaposition of the two family traditions heightens the sense of unreality. At her house, he feels lost in the chaos; at his house, she feels like people are sleepwalking.

This is but one example of the differences they bring to their marriage. Some are obvious, others less so. Sometimes, discovering a new area of difference can be a fascinating exploration that adds depth to the relationship. Sometimes, it's like stepping on a land mine.

In case you're wondering, that's a real case history—mine (Cameron's). I am Chinese-American. My mother was born in China and immigrated to the United States as a teenager. My father, also Chinese, was born here. Mom was an only child. Dad was the eldest of five, but the siblings had little to do with one another. Mom and Dad spoke different dialects, and therefore spoke only English at home. For the most part, my older sister and I were raised as middle-class suburban Americans with little connection to extended family and few Chinese friends.

My wife, of Palestinian descent, lived most of her childhood in Lebanon before immigrating to the United States as a teenager, as my mother had. And like my father, she is the eldest of five. Both Arabic and English were spoken in her home, often woven together in the same sentence. Her family remains part of a large but close-knit Arab American community, characterized by strong blood ties, loyalties, and obligations.

Born on opposite sides of the globe, we met in college—young, inexperienced, and naive. We fell in love, but not in the manner of Hollywood romances. We were two young adults who became friends and stumbled together through a relationship and into marriage, to the amusement of some and the alarm of others. Our coming together provoked reactions that uncovered the same tacit question on both sides: shouldn't people marry "their own kind"?

That was more than thirty years ago, and we're *still* discovering and dealing with the many differences of habit and expectation, cultural and otherwise, that we brought with us into the marriage. Things we never discussed had to be worked out, sometimes over a period of years, sometimes incompletely, and sometimes not at all. What's the husband's role in the family? The wife's? Who works? Who decides what's to be done with the money? What are our mutual obligations to extended family? How and when should children be disciplined?

In thinking about difference, I have always found both comfort and challenge in what Paul teaches about the body of Christ, in the twelfth chapter of both 1 Corinthians and Romans. The believers in Corinth were a contentious and divided lot; the Roman Christians were struggling with the tension between the Jewish minority and the Gentile majority, the former feeling shoved aside by the latter. But to all the believers in both cities, Paul had the same message: you are one body in Christ. The body has to have different parts that serve different functions. If it didn't, it wouldn't be a body; it would be a monstrosity. So face it: you need each other. And this is all by God's will and design.

There's much talk of *multiculturalism* and *diversity* these days. The technologies that connect us to a bewildering world of people and places, information and ideas, make it impossible to ignore the fact that others think differently from us. But what do we do with those differences? Tolerate them? Or actually learn to value and embrace them?

Paul certainly would not have wanted Jewish and Gentile believers just to tolerate each other. The divides of culture, status, and even gender had been overcome in the cross: "There is neither Jew nor Gentile, neither slave nor free, nor is there male and female, for you are all one in Christ Jesus" (Gal. 3:28).

One body; one flesh. What is true of Christians in general should also be true of Christian marriage, perhaps *especially* true. God intends marriage to be a true union based on love. Differences must be recognized and transcended; they should not be eliminated but rather accepted and sometimes even celebrated in a relationship grounded in grace.

This is a crucial point, so let us say it again in a different way. Every couple will have differences, which may be at the root of problems and conflicts that arise in the relationship, but *the differences themselves are not the problem*. In some cases, differ-

14

ences may lead to potentially solvable problems, as when spouses disagree on how the household finances are to be managed. In other cases, differences may result in the "perpetual issues" mentioned in the previous chapter. In such situations, spouses may need to learn to accept some things about each other that will never change. And the happy irony is that when they learn to do this, what once seemed like a constant source of annoyance may become just another fact of life.

Thus, each person brings a unique constellation of experiences and expectations to the union. At some point, a wife's expectations may clash with her husband's, even if both hail from the same culture. The tendency is to take one's own expectations for granted, such that the other person's perspective seems odd or even nonsensical. The attitude, whether it's said out loud or not, is often, "What's the matter with you? Why can't you see the *obvious*?" Unless spouses work past this self-centered stance, things are likely to go downhill from there.

In this book, we present the task of helping couples deal with difference as central to the task of preparing them for marriage. And as we suggested in chapter 1, a good place to start is with a healthy dose of realism regarding marriage itself.

Getting Real

People are more aware than ever that it takes work to keep a marriage relationship strong. Yet many Americans still cling to romantic ideals of marriage. We've seen it time and again on the silver screen. Boy meets girl, and they fall in love; then something threatens to destroy their relationship, but they persevere and come back together in the end. And when the credits roll and the theme music swells, everyone knows that the two will live happily ever after.

Or will they? What if the story kept going? On what would the stability and success of their relationship be based? They've heroically overcome impossible obstacles together—but will they survive the battle over whose turn it is to change Junior's diaper? What if Romeo and Juliet hadn't died at the end of Shakespeare's tragic play? Would the marriage have weathered their arguments over in-laws?

Some engaged couples are more idealistic than realistic. He thinks, *She has such a close relationship with God. I wish mine were like that. But after we're married, her spiritual life is bound to rub off on me.* Then they get married. Not only does he find himself in the same place spiritually as he was before, but also her use of religious language begins to grate on him, as if she were silently accusing him for his lack of growth.

She thinks, *He's so wonderfully independent. He knows his own mind and makes his own decisions. I can't talk to my parents like he does. But when we're married, he'll help me be strong.* Then they get married. He doesn't teach her how to be more independent of her parents; he just tells her to stop being a wimp. She feels pulled in two directions: can she be loyal to both her husband and her parents, without someone feeling betrayed?

Prospective partners may harbor almost magical expectations of how being married to the other will change their lives for the better. For example, in 2001, researchers at the National Marriage Project surveyed more than one thousand Americans in their twenties. Of the never-married singles in the group, men and women, 94 percent agreed with the statement that in marriage, "you want your spouse to be your soul mate, first and foremost." A full 88 percent agreed that their soul mate was "waiting for [them] somewhere out there," and nearly as many (87 percent) believed that when the time came to marry, they would indeed find that person.[1]

That's not to say that these twenty-somethings thought marriage was easy. Indeed, having grown up in the era when the divorce rate was at its peak, they were skeptical about marriage as an institution, even while craving the deep emotional connection that the idea of a soul mate seems to promise. But can marriage really live up to that billing? As Blaine Fowers has written, "The central fact in the history of marriage is that over the course of the past four centuries our expectations for fulfillment in this relationship have risen enormously."[2] Such expectations put tremendous pressure on a relationship. As one woman has admitted:

> Before Phil and I got married, I didn't spend a ton of time thinking about what marriage would be like. I had always heard, though, that marriage completes people, so I guess I believed that through marriage I would become spiritually and emotionally whole. I honestly don't know where I got that. But it was there in me—and big time. I also believed that being married, I would feel loved and adored at least 99 percent of the time. . . . Especially when we first got married, I wanted Phil to meet all my needs. It was as if the ring went on my finger and Phil went on my life pedestal. And because I had put him on mine, I wanted to be on his life pedestal, too.[3]

Unrecognized and unchallenged, expectations like these are guaranteed to bring disappointment and disillusionment, to which new spouses may react with anger or resentment, as if they had somehow been tricked.

Christians, moreover, are not exempt. The pseudospiritual language of soul mates lends itself well to Christianized versions of the ideal, as in, "Somewhere out there is the one person whom God has chosen for me from the beginning of time. I just have to find him or her." It's but one variation on an unrealistic theme: *if I just marry the right person, everything will be fine.*

Here's the unvarnished reality: even the best of marriages is still a flawed union between sinful people. In the flush of premarital enthusiasm, engaged couples may focus on the things that draw them together, and overlook the things that might push them apart. What seemed cute before the wedding may soon become downright annoying after.

Does that mean that there's no such thing as a happy marriage? Of course not. But regardless of whom one marries, it pays to anticipate that troublesome differences will crop up in every marriage. As we hope to make clear, it's not usually the differences themselves that are the problem. It's the way couples deal with them that matters.

We'll illustrate the point below with two of the most common areas in which couples struggle with differing expectations: gender and culture. Because there is so much that can be said about each area, we'll confine ourselves in this chapter to describing briefly some of the practical consequences of gender and culture differences for how couples communicate.

Different Planets, Different Worlds

In 1992, counselor John Gray wrote a best seller whose title has become a well-worn cultural trope: men are from Mars; women are from Venus.[4] Men and women have such different values and goals that people of the other gender may seem like they're from another planet. Here's how Gray describes what men want out of life: "Martians value power, competency, efficiency, and achievement. They are always doing things to prove themselves and develop their power and skills. Their sense of self is defined through their ability to achieve results. They experience fulfillment primarily through success and accomplishment."[5] Contrast that description with the corresponding stereotype of what women want: "Venusians have different values. They value love, communication, beauty, and relationships. They spend a lot of time supporting, helping, and nurturing one another. Their sense of self is defined through their feelings and the quality of their relationships. They experience fulfillment through sharing and relating."[6] Thus, a newlywed wife, for example, wishes that she and her husband would spend more time together; she remembers their courtship longingly. She asks her husband, "How come we never go out anymore?" He responds defensively, "That's not true; we go out sometimes." Internally, he reacts as if she had said, "I'm not happy, and you are therefore a failure as a husband." Her "Venusian" language of relationship needs to be translated into his "Martian" language of action: "I really want to have some fun together. Can we go out to dinner tonight?"

Some of Gray's ideas parallel those of an earlier best-selling work by linguist Deborah Tannen, who argued that "male-female conversation is cross-cultural communication."[7] Gender-based differences in values and conversational goals are socialized into children early on. Women want "rapport-talk" that serves connection and intimacy; men want information-based "report-talk" that helps them keep up their status in a social hierarchy. Thus, when a wife wants to connect with her husband and tells him that she "just wants to talk," he sits down ready for a conversation. But he may be thoroughly confused if he finds that she doesn't already have something specific she needs to talk *about* in order to solve a problem!

Variations on the theme abound. Emerson Eggerichs, for example, uses Paul—"each one of you also must love his wife as he loves himself, and the wife must respect her husband" (Eph. 5:33)—to argue that above all, wives need love from their husbands, while husbands need respect from their wives.[8] Others have made similar observations. Shaunti Feldhahn tells of a retreat where the speaker divided the audience by gender and then asked everyone to make a hypothetical choice: would he or she rather feel unloved or disrespected? The women gasped when nearly every man in the room preferred being unloved to being disrespected; the men were equally flummoxed when the women made the opposite choice.[9]

unloved vs disrespected

Critics accuse such authors of creating simplistic gender stereotypes.[10] Though many men and women fit these descriptions, not all do. We personally know couples in which the roles are reversed: the women are the problem-solvers, and their husbands complain when they feel their wives aren't listening. The fact is, many of the presumed differences between men and women simply don't hold up well to empirical scrutiny—certainly not at the level of suggesting that they're from different planets! As a whole, men and women are more alike than different. There's no denying, however, the best-selling appeal of these ideas or their ability to transform how husbands and wives understand each other and their marriage.

The same happens when couples begin to discover their cultural differences. Some differences may be obvious: physical appearance, language, or food customs. But culture is also the source of deeply and unconsciously held norms and values that affect relationships in surprising and perplexing ways:

> We usually cannot clearly describe the rules of our culture. But these complex and largely invisible cultural codes permeate every aspect of our beliefs and behavior and are primal in their power. . . . They have a profound influence on our attitudes about money and work, what kind of behavior we consider to be on time or late, eating habits, child rearing and discipline, flirting and sex, small talk and big talk, why and how we get angry, or how we apologize.[11]

Invisible, ubiquitous, and primal in their power: is it any wonder that cultural differences can lead to unfortunate misinterpretations and conflict between spouses?

Take conversational distance as an example. People who come from different backgrounds often have different comfort zones in terms of how closely two people in a conversation should stand. Across many cultures, it's normal to stand further from strangers than from family, friends, or people in whom you're romantically interested. But cultures vary in terms of where these zones fall. What feels close to one person may feel distant to another, leading to misinterpretation of the other's intentions.

Psychologist Joel Crohn tells the story of Marla and Jorge, who met at a party, fell in love, and later got engaged. She was a native Californian with a middle-class Irish background; he grew up in Mexico as part of an upper-middle-class family. As Marla remembers their first conversation, Jorge stood close to her, signaling that he was interested in her. She responded by lightly touching his arm, which he took as signaling her interest in *him*. But in Jorge's mind, Marla was the one who took the initiative by touching him; he had kept a respectful distance! Neither had recognized their own unconscious rules of social distance. Not surprisingly, at a later party, Marla went ballistic when she saw Jorge standing too close to another woman, while he again thought he was keeping himself at a neutral and honorable distance. The misunderstanding nearly cost them their relationship.[12]

Gender and culture, of course, can't be neatly separated, since culture shapes what we think it means to be a man or a woman. But the point is that we come to every relationship preloaded with a set of assumptions about what's "right" or "normal." When those assumptions operate invisibly, we may think the other person is simply wrong and being stubborn about it, while we remain blissfully unaware of what *we* bring to the conflict.

Simple and stereotypical distinctions such as "Mars versus Venus" are powerful because they can provoke a shift in perspective. For many couples, reading such books is an epiphany—"Holy cow! *That's* why my husband is the way he is! *That's* why my wife talks the way she does! We're normal!" It helps them calm down and approach their differences more generously.

But even though stereotypes can help couples move toward mutual understanding and acceptance, they can also blind them to more complex realities or become ways to justify unfair behavior. John Gray, for example, writes of how stressed-out husbands need to retreat into their "cave" to calm down.[13] Gray's discussion includes some truly cringe-worthy stereotypes: "To expect a man who is in his cave instantly to become open, responsive, and loving is as unrealistic as expecting a woman who is upset immediately to calm down and make complete sense. It is a mistake to expect a man to always be in touch with his loving feelings just as it is a mistake to expect a woman's feelings to always be rational and logical."[14] If that advice sounds sensible, in part it's because of his use of extreme words such as *instantly, immediately, complete,* and *always*. But take those words out and reread the passage. It's easy to imagine how such stereotypes could actually encourage men, for example, to think, *Don't bother me—I have to go to my cave!*

Dealing constructively with differences requires a new way of thinking. Spouses need help getting past the cycle of blaming each other for problems in their marriage. It's not about one or the other person being odd or obstinate. Most of the time, it's about two normal people who happen to be different from each other and are still learning to accept those differences.

Learning to Think in Relational Terms

When it comes to understanding their marital conflicts, couples—and the people who want to help them—need to learn to think *systemically*, that is, to think in relational rather than individual terms. Here's a metaphor your elementary school science teacher would love. When you put vinegar and baking soda together, you get a mess. But that doesn't mean there's something "wrong" with either ingredient by itself. It's the combination that results in something new and potentially explosive. The vinegar can't "blame" the soda, or vice versa.

We're not saying that there's no such thing as blameworthy behavior. But human beings have a tendency to give themselves the benefit of the doubt and believe that the blame for conflict lies primarily with the other person. And when both parties do this in righteous indignation, it makes for a downward spiral of accusation and defensiveness that's hard to break. See if any of these self-justifying interpretations sound familiar:

- If I don't hear something you say, it's because you didn't say it clearly. But if you don't hear something I say, it's because you never listen to me.

- If I lose my temper with you, it's because anyone in my situation would have done the same thing. But if you lose your temper with me, it's because you have a problem with anger.

- If I forget our anniversary, it's because I've been really busy. But if you forget our anniversary, it's because you don't care.

These are examples of what social psychologists call the "fundamental attribution error," a self-serving bias in how people interpret their own behavior as opposed to someone else's. If *I* have a difficulty, then the *situation* must be to blame. But if *you* have a difficulty, it's because of a deficit in your *character*.[15] Not that I would say that out loud—I might even pride myself on having the self-control to hold back what I'm really thinking!

When couples confront the differences between them, they bring this biased way of thinking to the interaction. My way is normal; yours is odd. I'm just responding; you started it. Neither partner is all that interested in listening to and understanding the other. The couple's energies go toward defending themselves or trying to correct each other.

Couples need to go beyond the way of thinking that makes marriage a competition of my way versus your way. It begins with what our colleague Terry Hargrave has called "the essential humility of marriage," in which stable and loving couples have transcended the mere "me" and "you" to create a sense of "us" together in marriage.[16] Individual differences still exist. But where the sense of "us-ness" is strong, individual partners sacrifice and compromise for the sake of the union, and do so willingly.

 When you help couples prepare for marriage, you have the privilege of working with them proactively to build that sense of partnership. Your task is to help them get beyond a "What's wrong with you?" or even "What's wrong with me?" way of thinking and reacting, to "Who do *we* want to be?" instead. They do this by confronting their differences calmly, and humbly submitting themselves to the discipline of constructive communication.

We'll discuss those skills in detail in chapter 4. Before we do that, however, we'll overview the context in which you'll teach couples those skills, by walking you through the structure of a flexible four-session process that revolves around a tool we call the "Conversation Jumpstarter."

Using the *Conversation Jumpstarter*: A Flexible Four-Session Framework

Education is part of the church's DNA. From Bible studies in someone's living room to marriage seminars in the fellowship hall, we excel at putting together events, big and small, that gather people together to learn. And there's solid evidence that premarital education classes work. They get couples off on the right foot by helping them learn new skills, and those who have been in such programs report improved relationships.[1]

But researchers are a cautious lot. They warn, for example, that we don't have hard evidence for long-term effects. In other words, a couple may say that a premarital workshop has been beneficial to them—but will those benefits last them all the way through those turbulent early years of marriage, when the risk of divorce is highest? Frankly, we just don't know yet.

In the meantime, we must do the best we can to prepare couples for marriage. We need not only to teach couples communication skills but also help them put those skills to use in real-life situations.[2] Workshops don't always accomplish this, since it takes the kind of individualized attention that is often difficult to achieve in a larger group setting. Meeting with one couple at a time is a much better environment for helping them put practical skills to realistic use.

That's what the Conversation Jumpstarter is all about. (Throughout the book, we may refer to the inventory as the "CJ" or the "Jumpstarter" for short.) It's the tool we've created to help you prepare couples for marriage. The idea is to have the bride and groom, separately at first, reflect on their values and past experiences in six common areas of conflict. This becomes the basis for conversations that help them uncover their own expectations of married life, while listening to and understanding each other's. Along the way, your job is to coach them to apply relationship skills successfully to the differences that the CJ has brought to the surface.

You'll find a reproducible copy of the Conversation Jumpstarter in appendix A. Take a few moments to begin familiarizing yourself with it now. Read the instructions and glance through the questions. Indeed, if you're married, we would highly recommend that you work through the CJ with your spouse after you've finished reading this book. Your own experience will give you both insight into and empathy for the couples with whom you work.

The Jumpstarter is organized into six broad sections corresponding to later chapters in this book: family roles and responsibilities; affection; money; children and parenting; relationships to extended family; and spirituality and devotion. Each chapter will give you a basic grounding in the topic and includes suggestions surrounding the specific questions in the CJ.

Many other topics, of course, could be covered. The point is not to ferret out every possible difference between the bride and groom. Even if that were possible, new differences would eventually emerge. The Jumpstarter therefore neither covers every possible topic nor each of its six topics in meticulous detail. Moreover, in the flexible four-session structure below you may not even cover all six topics, depending on the decisions you make as their coach.

The process we are recommending is thus not one of comprehensive diagnosis and problem solving. The point, rather, is to give couples a positive, successful experience of (a) taking ownership of their own individual expectations, even ones they may not have been aware of before, (b) bringing those expectations into conversations with their partner, (c) being able to listen to what their partner says while staying calm, and (d) working toward mutual understanding in a way that strengthens their unity. This will give them hope that it's possible to face their differences without fear.

Here, then, are the suggested steps for using the CJ. This chapter will give you an overview of the process; for your convenience, an outline of the process can be found at the end of the chapter. More specific guidance on coaching the conversations will be given in chapter 6. You will need a brief initial meeting to get the process started and to orient the couple to the Jumpstarter. After that, you will meet with the couple four times, in ninety-minute sessions.

The Orientation Meeting: Give the Couple the *Conversation Jumpstarter*

Have an initial meeting with the couple to orient them to the CJ and to the preparation process as a whole. This would be a good time to clarify your role with them, since some of the couples you work with may be wondering how the process differs from pastoral counseling. Be clear in your own mind how this ministry relates to your other roles, set appropriate boundaries between them, and communicate this to the couple.

At your discretion, the discussion may range over a variety of areas, from personal small talk to your church's official wedding policy, so the amount of time needed will vary. Overall, though, the goal is for everyone to finish the meeting with a clear understanding of what's expected of whom in the process. Make sure the couple knows that the success of the preparation process will depend in large part on whether they take their homework seriously.

Give the couple two copies of the inventory; this will be the homework assignment they must complete before your first full meeting. Read through the instructions aloud with them, insert your own comments as needed, and tell them to read the instructions again before they begin writing. The assignment will take time, and we don't recommended trying to plow through the entire Jumpstarter in one sitting. The instructions therefore encourage the more relaxed pace of doing one section per day. Many couples, of course, have such packed schedules that this way of doing it will sound too time-consuming. Don't insist; encourage. Help them understand that now is as good a time as any to start figuring out how to make time for the things that matter!

To that end, make sure they have at least a week to complete the task. Let them know that the assignment is not a test with right and wrong answers, but more like writing in a journal. If they think of something else relevant after they've already responded to a question, they're free to go back and add it.

When they've completed the CJ, they're each to make two copies of their answers, keeping the original and one copy for themselves, and delivering the other copy to you. Thus you will have a copy of everything that both the bride and the groom have written. Encourage them to hold off discussing their answers until you can all meet together to do so in a safe and orderly way. Of course, their curiosity or anxiety may get the best of them; if they later tell you that they couldn't help themselves and talked about it, just accept the fact and move on.

In terms of timing, it's always best if marriage preparation can be finished well before the wedding—ideally, before the invitations go out. Otherwise, couples who begin to have serious doubts about marrying may see no graceful way to cancel or postpone the wedding, and may go ahead with it to avoid an awkward confrontation with family and friends.

Keep that in mind when deciding whether to work with a couple. Will there be enough time to do the process properly? After the orientation meeting, you'll need a minimum of five weeks, depending on everyone's availability: one for the couple to complete the Jumpstarter, one for you to review their answers before your first meeting, and three more for the remaining meetings. Before you finish the orientation meeting, get your calendars out. Give the couple a deadline for when you need their answers in hand, and schedule the first session for at least one week after that. Schedule the remaining three sessions at weekly intervals or longer, advising them that they will have homework to do between sessions.

Preparing for the First Session: Carefully and Thoughtfully Read Their Answers

Depending on the couple, there may be quite a bit of reading to do! Make sure you've scheduled enough time to read their answers with full attention and to form your own impressions of where the trouble spots might be. Sometimes, this will be fairly obvious. If one partner states a concrete expectation and the other states a clearly contradictory one, this is an obvious candidate for discussion—though not until the couple has had a chance to experience some success in using the communication skills you've taught them.

Even where there is no clear contradiction, a minor disagreement can balloon into a fight if it touches a sore spot or traumatic memory. The groom may have grown up in a financially reckless family. The bride didn't and is therefore more flexible on saving and spending. But her lack of a firm and passionate commitment to saving for the future may trigger what seems like unreasonable anxiety in her fiancé. She may need help listening to why this is so important to him, while he may need help understanding why she doesn't share his anxiety.

Here's one more wrinkle: people will not always make their feelings obvious. They may recount horrific stories of abuse with perfect calm and no overt emotion; it's one way of defending against feelings that might otherwise overwhelm them. So use your intuition. If you read a story in their answers that *you* think would be traumatic, make a mental note of it.

They will be soon be reading and responding to each other's answers, so your preliminary assessment of what they've written is simply one voice in the conversation, not the last word. All you're doing at this point is forming tentative hypotheses about which topic areas would be most sensitive or important to discuss.

The First Session: Have Them Tell Their Story and Teach Them to Communicate

Your first meeting with the couple will have two parts. In the first part, after you've exchanged pleasantries and they're comfortably seated, say, "Tell me how the two of you met, and how you decided to get married." Alternatively, if they haven't yet decided but are only exploring the possibility of marriage, you can say something like, "Tell me how the two of you met and what it is about your relationship now that leads you to think about getting married."

Recall the distinction between content and process: the point of the storytelling task is to give the couple an easy way to begin talking so that you can observe the process. It's not that content isn't important; if they're only getting married because she's pregnant, you need to know that! But your focus will be more on the *how* than the *what*, the process as opposed to the content.

Observe how they tell the story. Are they playful and affectionate, or tense and competitive? Do they both contribute to the tale, or does one partner seem to be the official storyteller? How do they deal with disagreements over the details? How well does each partner receive correction from the other? Paying attention to the process in this way will help you know some of the strengths and weaknesses of the relationship.

In the second part of the session, your role is more didactic; you will be teaching them the crucial skills of listening and speaking to each other, using the "Constructive Communication" handout in appendix B. Many otherwise loving relationships break down because of a lack of skill. Small differences can turn into gaping rifts when one person isn't listening, or is speaking in a way that puts the other on the defensive. We'll describe the skills themselves in the next chapter.

At the end of the first session, give them each *six copies* of the "Responding to My Partner's Answers" handout found in appendix C. Remind them that they will each need to bring two things to the next scheduled session: (a) their personal copy of the Constructive Communication handout, and (b) their completed homework assignment. These will be the basis for the session.

Homework. Earlier, each partner made two copies of his or her answers to the CJ. One copy went to you. The other now goes to the opposite partner. Taking one topic at a time, they are to read each other's answers—*privately*—and respond to them in writing, using one copy of the "Responding" handout for each of the six topics. On the top of each page, they write their name and the name of the topic. In the spaces provided, they then write whatever thoughts they have regarding (a) what they like about their partner's answer, (b) what they have further questions about, and (c) what worries them. Finally, they rate how important each topic is to them personally, and how difficult they think it will be to discuss.

The Second Session: Help Them Practice Constructive Communication

At the beginning of the session, check to make sure they've done their homework. If they haven't, we would recommend rescheduling. Help them understand the reason: preparing for marriage is essentially *their* work, not yours. You're not the one getting married!

As mentioned earlier, some couples will already have jumped in to discuss their answers, before meeting with you. Don't be alarmed if they tell you that their conversations haven't gone well. Simply listen compassionately but matter-of-factly to what they say, and reinforce the idea that good communication skills take practice, which is the point of your meeting together. Use their experience as leverage to motivate them to learn.

The first task for the session is for the three of you to use their homework to do a quick evaluation of the degree of difficulty of the six topics. Couples need an early experience of success, and starting with less explosive subjects helps. Anything rated as both "important" and "difficult" by either partner will be more challenging. Have them look at their ratings. Which topics shouldn't be a problem? Which might get tense? Agree together on which two topics would be the easiest to discuss, and which two the hardest. Choose one of the easy topics as the basis for the session; the other easy one will be the basis of their homework.

For the remainder of the session, you will help them practice the skills you taught them in the first session. Take a few minutes to walk them back through the handout on constructive communication (have copies of the handout available in case they've forgotten to bring theirs). Then have them face each other. Choose someone to be the first speaker. Encourage both of them to refer to the handout as needed as they apply the skills to the following exercise.

The exercise has three phases. Essentially, you will coach them through three short and parallel mini-conversations based on their written homework responses: first, what they liked about their partner's answers; then, what they had a question about; and finally, what worried or concerned them. In each conversation, your job is not to help them resolve any questions or differences but merely to coach them to stay within the constructive communication guidelines.

Let's say the bride is chosen to be the first speaker, making the groom the listener. In the first conversation, referring to her homework, the bride briefly tells the groom one thing she liked about his answers to the topic at hand, while he listens. If the first topic is parenting, for example, she might say, "I was really happy to read that you just want a couple of kids. Me too! I was worried because we've never talked about it, and we both came from big families." For now, don't let her say much more than that, because he has to take in what she's saying and respond.

He then says back in his own words, as accurately as possible and without judgment, what he heard her say: "You were glad to find out that I don't want a big family. You were worried that I might." As in normal conversation, she may have other things to say, but coach her to keep her comments related to the previous interchange. Each time she speaks, help her follow the principles of constructive communication as needed, and help the husband to listen.

After a few exchanges, they switch roles. He is now the speaker, telling her something he liked about her answer, while she listens. Again, continue to coach them to communicate constructively. Depending on how much they wrote in the "what I like" section, they can go back and forth, alternating in the roles of speaker and listener.

The second conversation will probably be longer. The bride might say, "I wondered about your checking the box that said you weren't close to your mom or your dad. That's really hard for me to understand. Do you still feel that way?" The groom must demonstrate that he's heard the question: "You want to know if I still feel the same way about my parents as I did back then." For the sake of practice and skill development, he should check his understanding this way, even if the question seems obvious. When she agrees that he's understood the question, he becomes the speaker and answers the question, while she switches into a listening mode.

Depending on the nature of the question, it may take a few conversational exchanges before she has understood his response—whether she *agrees* with it or not. When this happens, the roles are reversed. It's his turn to ask a question, and the conversation proceeds as before. How many turns they take will be up to you; remember, there's still one more conversation to go.

The third mini-conversation has the same structure as the previous one, except this time, the bride begins with one of her concerns: "What worried me was something you wrote in the last section. It sounds like your father was pretty harsh when he punished you, and I'm worried about what will happen with our own kids." Realistically, the conversation regarding worries should be relatively mild if the topic is truly an easy one. Still, you should expect this conversation (and others like it in future sessions) to provoke a bit more anxiety. Partners are likely to be more defensive, requiring a firmer hand from you as a coach.

It's impossible to predict exactly where any of these conversations will go. Stay alert and active as a coach, remembering that the purpose of the exercise is not to solve problems but to improve the couple's skill at conversational turn taking. Your job, using the three mini-conversation structure, is to (a) coach them to use constructive communication skills, and (b) enforce the simple principle that one doesn't get to be the speaker until the other feels heard.

When all three conversations are finished, debrief the experience with them. What did they find most helpful about the exercise? What was the most difficult? What, if anything, did they learn about themselves or their relationship? As you debrief, make sure to practice good listening skills yourself, showing that you understand their concerns without having to fix them. Exercises like this, especially when dealing with more difficult topics or surprising information, can leave them a little unsettled. That's normal, and can motivate them to reflect more deeply on the relationship. As long as they've been able to listen successfully to each other, and you don't see signs that they need to be referred to a counselor (see chapter 1), there's no cause for alarm.

[handwritten margin note: # at the end of each session]

Couples will vary tremendously in terms of how much coaching they need to complete the exercise successfully. Some will finish quickly; if so, it isn't necessary to continue the session for the full ninety minutes. Many, however, will need the full time, so stress the importance of punctuality. Budget fifteen minutes at the beginning for choosing the topics, and fifteen minutes for debriefing at the end. That leaves about an hour for the communication exercise—and you may need to be a very directive coach to accomplish the task in that amount of time!

Homework. A successfully managed conversation in the second session becomes the foundation for the couple to begin practicing constructive communication skills on their own. Earlier, you chose two "easy" topics, and used one. The other topic now becomes the basis for their homework. Essentially, they will do the same turn-taking exercise they did in their session with you but with the other easy topic and without your coaching. Give them a copy of the "Practice Communication Exercise" handout from appendix D. The handout is self-explanatory; familiarize yourself with it before giving it to them. Walk through the handout together and answer any questions. They must complete the exercise before the next session.

27

The Third Session: Check In, Continue Practicing, and Then Go to the Next Step

Your third full session with the couple will have three parts. First, check in with the couple to make sure that they have done their homework. Find out what went well, and what could have gone better. Stay positive. If necessary, remind them again that it takes time and practice to learn new skills. If they tell you that their conversation got stuck, go back and coach them through it. Again, we'll say more about coaching in chapter 6, but here's the basic idea.

Don't replay the entire homework exercise. Ask them to remember where the discussion broke down and then *show* you what happened. Watch specifically for places where their communication gets derailed, and get them quickly back on track. Remind them that at this point, it's not about trying to resolve conflict but to practice communication; the exercise is successful if they both felt heard by the other, even if they still disagree. Consider referring them to a counselor if you can't coach them through the impasse.

The second part of your meeting repeats the mini-conversation exercise, this time using a topic with a slightly higher degree of difficulty. Thus, again, the bride and groom take turns speaking and listening as they tell each other what they appreciated, what they had questions about, and what they were worried about regarding this new topic. Your job, as before, is to coach them to stay on track with constructive communication skills throughout.

It's possible that by the time the exercise is finished, you have little time left in your session. If so, don't start something new that you can't finish. Instruct them to repeat the mini-conversation exercise with the next topic, and begin the following session by checking in with them and coaching them through any difficulties, as before.

But if you still have at least thirty minutes left, you will need to make a decision about what you will do from here to the end of the final session. Through coaching them, you've been able to observe how comfortable they are in using the skills. The question now is this: should you continue on the same path, giving them more practice, or teach them something new? Here are three possibilities.

Option 1: Continue practicing communication. It never hurts to practice the fundamentals. Even professional athletes continue to work diligently honing their skills, embedding them in "muscle memory" so that they become more and more automatic. Similarly, you don't just want couples to succeed at a couple of exercises; you want them to integrate the skills into who they are and into their life together.

Option 1, therefore, is to keep doing what you've already been doing: have them practice their skills with mini-conversations around a new topic, with you and/or at home. This is probably the best option if (a) it seems to you that the couple is still uncomfortable with the skills, or (b) for a time at least, *you* are uncomfortable with the other options! Rest assured, however, that we believe option 1 would still be of benefit to any couple.

Option 2: Discuss ways to be proactive about conflict. For options 2 and 3, we're assuming that you're reasonably confident in the couple's skills. Consider adding to their repertoire by helping them avoid unnecessary conflict. As we will describe in chapter 5, there are two ways to go about this, and you can use your remaining time exploring one or both strategies. The first involves teaching the couple the importance of positive, relationship-affirming behaviors. Using appendix E, "Making Our Marriage Stronger," you coach them through a conversation that helps them identify behaviors that communicate appreciation and acceptance, and plan how to maintain those behaviors in their relationship.

The second is to help them recognize the negative "dance" they may typically fall into that signals the beginning of a conflict. By helping them notice and discuss the steps of the dance, you create the basis for talking about how they will help each other stop it before it gets out of control. This conversation works best if you've already observed the pattern, but you will also coach them to make their own observations and arrive at their own insights.

Option 3: Teach them how to make decisions in the face of conflicting needs. This option also assumes that the couple is relatively at ease with constructive communication. However, during your conversations a practical impasse may have cropped up, and a concrete decision is needed. She wants to keep all their money in joint bank accounts; he wants to keep money in separate accounts. She wants to spend Christmas with her family on the East Coast; he wants to be with his family on the West Coast.

In such situations, it would be helpful to teach them a method of creative problem solving. The method itself, which is also described further in chapter 5, gives couples a safer structure in which to explore possible solutions to the conflict. Note that the procedure is best learned when (a) there is an actual decision the couple needs to make as to what to do in a specific situation and (b) they have conflicting ideas, needs, or desires relative to that decision.

If this option seems appropriate, you can make an observation such as the following: "Earlier, when you were talking about relating to your respective families, the question of where you're going to spend Christmas came up. If it's OK with you, I'd like to use that situation to walk you through a way of making that kind of decision that's less likely to end in a fight."

Give them a copy of appendix F, "Making Decisions When Our Needs Conflict." Coach them through each step until they've come up with a plan. Debrief: what was it like for them to discuss the problem this way, relative to how they may have tried to solve similar dilemmas in the past? If their experience seems to have been positive, ask them if they have another decision to which they might apply the method, and if so, you can make that their homework. Be sure to check in with them at the beginning of the next session.

Other options. We've designed the process with plenty of flexibility in mind. As their coach, you're in charge of how the time in each session will be spent. Use your judgment. Do what seems right for the couple you have in front of you. Helping them have an experience of relationship success is far more important than trying to push through a prearranged plan.

The Fourth Session: Put It All Together and Debrief

What you do in the fourth session depends on the choices you made in the third. Always begin by asking how the homework went, congratulating them on their success or coaching them through any difficulties. For the remainder of the session, do what seems most needful. Not sure what that is? Ask them; by this time, they should be fully engaged in the process, with a better sense of what they need than when they began.

Couples need to be challenged in order to grow. In the process described, this happens through increasing the difficulty of the conversations and adding new exercises and skills. But always go at their pace, increasing the intensity of your coaching involvement as needed so that they don't get discouraged. Hopefully, by the time they finish the final session, they will have had at least one experience of discussing something difficult while communicating well.

Be sure to leave at least twenty minutes at the end of the session to debrief the whole process. What have they learned about themselves and their relationship? What will they do with that knowledge going forward? Encourage them not to throw away their responses to the CJ; they can use them to start new conversations on their own. Finally, if needed, you can also discuss whether additional sessions or a referral to a counselor are wanted or warranted.

And Beyond . . .

There may be many more things you want to discuss with the couple, from the importance of Christian love and commitment to the politics of the invitation list. It's up to the three of you to decide how many times to meet beyond the orientation plus four-session structure we've outlined, and what purpose those meetings would serve.

Should you do more sessions? More practice of skills never hurts. But consider first whether any progress has been made. Remember that your task is to provide an experience of success that becomes the foundation of a hopeful outlook toward the future. If there are to be further sessions, it should be because all of you agree that the couple is on a positive trajectory already, and that continuing to work together will add to their sense of readiness for marriage.

You should already have a pretty good idea of what the three of you can accomplish together. No pastor or coach can help everyone. Be honest with yourself and with the couple. Don't keep working with them on the off chance that something good might happen. If what you're doing isn't helping, it would be better to refer.

As the result of their sessions, some couples may recognize that even what should have been easy discussions were fraught with difficulty, and they may decide either to delay or even cancel the wedding. From the standpoint of a ministry that seeks to strengthen marriage, helping people to be wiser about relationship choices in this way can be a successful outcome. But not everyone will see it that way. You may end up taking some heat from family members who will cast you as the villain for breaking up a beautiful wedding!

In summary, these are the steps we would recommend for using the Jumpstarter to prepare couples for marriage. Feel free to modify the structure as needed to fit your own ministry and ways of working. Just keep the overall goal in mind: to give engaged couples both the relationship skills they will need in order to deal with their differences, and the experience of actually using them successfully with potentially troublesome issues. The next three chapters will describe what these skills are and guide you in helping couples to apply them.

The *Conversation Jumpstarter*:
An Outline of the Process

Orientation.   Discuss roles; give Jumpstarter to couple.

Preparation.   Read their responses.

Session 1.   Couple tells story of how they met; teach constructive communication.

Homework: Couple responds to each other's CJ.

Session 2.   Practice communication through coached mini-conversations.

Homework: Mini-conversations without coaching.

Session 3.   Debrief homework; continue coached practice.

Options: Continue practice; coach proactive positivity or decision-making. Assign related homework.

Session 4.   Debrief homework; coach a relevant exercise; debrief process.

Part Two

Constructive Communication

Chapter Four

Communication That Builds Relationship

Marriage brings together two people into what will hopefully be a lifelong covenant union. Because they come with different histories, they may also differ in deeply rooted beliefs that they've learned from their cultures and families of origin. The possible stumbling blocks are legion. They may have many expectations of which they are unaware, and when these are violated, they feel as bewildered as if gravity itself had been reversed. A destructive cycle of blame and resentment often follows.

Marriage preparation, however, is not about getting rid of these differences of belief and expectation, any more than discipleship is about getting Christians to have the same spiritual gift. True unity is not founded on sameness but on the humble ability to accept and even to celebrate difference. Couples need the skills to avoid or break the negative cycles that might otherwise be triggered by their differences. As Clifford Notarius and Howard Markman have written:

> It's not the differences between partners that cause problems but how the differences are handled when they arise. . . . [P]artners in happy relationships develop good listening skills. These skills have nothing to do with eliminating differences, forcing consensus, or giving advice. Listening skills involve understanding and acceptance of differences in personality and taste.[1]

For the stability and success of their marriage, the question is not whether the bride-to-be and her beau *have* differences; the question is whether they possess the skills to handle those differences constructively. Your job is to teach these skills and to help couples apply them to conversations about real-life differences.

Fair warning: many couples will complain, "It's not natural; real people don't talk this way." But real people can also hurt each other by doing what comes "naturally." Any new skill is awkward at first; one suffers some dents and dings before driving becomes second nature.

Another objection may be raised: "There can't be just one 'right' way to communicate!" Agreed. Constructive communication is our proposed means to a desired end; the goal is a marriage characterized by mutual understanding and acceptance. If couples already have a way of communicating that builds unity even when confronted with difference, then by all means encourage them to do *that*!

In casual conversation, two people may joke, laugh, and tell stories; they enjoy the camaraderie without worrying much about who's really listening or how things are being said. And if, at the dinner table, a wife says to her husband, "Please pass the salt," he can simply hand her the saltshaker without having to say, "The food's a little bland, and you'd like some salt."

But, it's too easy to assume that all conversation should go that way—that we should just be able to say things without having to think too much first, and have the right things happen without being misunderstood. It often works that way, but not always—and it's the exceptions that cause the fractures in a marriage.

As described in the previous chapter, you will be teaching constructive communication skills in your first session. The skills should be thought of as tools that couples pick up and use when they need them. Building a successful marriage requires intentionality; you work toward a goal, choosing the right tools for the job. This is particularly important when strong emotions are involved, when just responding by reflex is most likely to get the couple into trouble. Trust us on this one: as they begin to practice and get competent at the skills, they will find that they need them much more often than they would have imagined at first! But first things first. Before teaching them to communicate, you must help them learn to stay calm.

Calm Down before Having or Continuing Difficult Discussions

Conversation happens. Much of the time, it's relatively effortless; spouses exchange information, make simple requests, or swap stories about their respective days. They don't draw upon any special skills; they just talk. But it's how spouses handle the more *difficult* conversations that matters most for the long-term success of the marriage. Destructive cycles of conflict can be triggered by nothing more than a word, a tone of voice, or a look.

It helps to understand a little of the physiology of conflict. People in a heightened emotional state have stress hormones such as adrenaline and cortisol coursing through their bodies, increasing their heart rate and blood pressure.[2] This is part of the "fight, flight, or freeze" response in which one feels that survival itself is on the line, making it difficult to remain calm, think clearly, or communicate well, even when one supposedly has the skill.

At first, couples may be tempted to believe that they are calmer than they really are and doggedly push through an argument, thinking, *We can do this*. That's risky, especially in the early stages of marriage when they need experiences of success to build up their confidence. Encourage them to give themselves the best chance of using their skills constructively by paying attention to the signs that tell them they need to calm down first.

As you begin the second half of your first session, give them each a copy of the "Constructive Communication" handout from appendix B. Ask them if they can tell when they're getting stressed out. What are the warning signs? Do they feel their hearts beating harder and faster?[3] Do their hands get cold and clammy? Do their stomachs churn or their necks get tense? Do they feel like running away? (Answer the question for yourself, and offer your own examples.) After a brief discussion, have them write their top two or three warning signs on their handout as a reminder.

Another method is to monitor finger temperature. As part of the fight-or-flight response, the body restricts blood flow to the hands and feet; that's why some people get cold hands when they're anxious. Thus, a simple test is to put your hands to your face, palms inward. If they feel cold, you're probably under stress.[4] The point is to encourage couples to be wise by not forcing a difficult conversation when they're having trouble staying calm. That one piece of advice would probably make for better conversations even without constructive communication skills!

If they're stressed out and emotions are on a hair trigger, it's time to take a break. The handout reminds them of four easy-to-explain rules.

First, either person can call for a time-out, even if the other person doesn't need one, because it only takes one anxious person to spark a negative spiral. The person calling for the time-out should avoid saying blameful things such as, "You're really stressing me out," and focus on his or her own need instead: "I'm feeling really stressed-out, and I need to take a break before I lose it." For the calmer person to agree to the other's need for a break is a way of showing concern for the other as well as for the marriage.

Second, taking a break is not a way to escape or avoid the issue. Before walking away, the partners should agree to a time and place to come back and try again. Since it may be difficult at that moment for them to negotiate even *that*, help them come up with a prearranged strategy, such as both spouses returning to the living room couch in half an hour.

Third, the break should be at least twenty minutes.[5] The spouses may start feeling calmer as soon as they get away from the conflict, but their physiological state may not have returned to normal. The lower their level of cardiovascular fitness, the longer it may take.

Finally, it won't help them calm down if they spend the break time nursing a grudge or mentally rehearsing their grievances. Ask them what kinds of activities help them to actually *relax*—recognizing that some recreational activities, like video games and some forms of music, actually get people *more* hyped-up emotionally instead of less.

Just as important are the things they say to themselves during the time-out. Like the Israelites murmuring in the desert, muttering negative thoughts will only make them more upset. *Why did I marry him?* and *She can't treat me that way* don't help. In place of these, John Gottman suggests more soothing thoughts such as the following:

- "Calm down. Take some deep breaths."
- "No need to take this personally."
- "There are lots of things I admire about him (her)."
- "Right now I'm upset, but this is basically a good marriage."[6]

In addition, Christian couples can approach the time-out in a spirit of prayer. Point them to appropriate passages of Scripture that they can read or prayerfully recite from memory. Rehearsing thoughts and short petitions like the following may also help:

- "God loves me. And God loves him [or her], too."
- "Lord, teach me to be the compassionate, patient, and humble person you want me to be."
- "Help me listen."

Hopefully, by the time they return to the conversation, they'll be calmer and more receptive.

Putting constructive communication skills to good use requires a more relational way of thinking: *If there's a problem of communication between us, what am I bringing to the relationship? What can I do to make us stronger? Instead of accusing my spouse of not listening, could I speak in ways that would make it easier for my spouse to hear me? Instead of resenting the way my spouse speaks to me, how can I be a better listener?*

In that spirit, here are two profound yet simple principles to teach your couples: *listen in a way that helps your partner feel heard*, and *speak in a way that makes it easier to listen*. Many misunderstandings and conflicts could be more easily solved or avoided if both partners followed these two principles consistently.

Listen in a Way That Helps Your Partner Feel Heard

Everyone wants to be heard. But that doesn't mean everyone wants to listen.

Many Christians know the verse, "Everyone should be quick to listen, slow to speak and slow to become angry, because human anger does not produce the righteousness that God desires" (James 1:19-20). The very same Christians, unfortunately, may get it exactly backward in daily life. They are quick to become angry with their spouses, quick to blurt out impulsive words, and slow to listen—and the same is true of their non-Christian friends. That's unfortunate, because the simple act of attentive listening can turn even difficult arguments in a more positive direction, and doing it habitually can change the course of a relationship.

It doesn't have to be complicated. For example, in the popular marriage curriculum known as *World Class Marriage*, participants are taught a simple form of listening that requires nothing more than facing the other person and occasionally nodding or inserting short quasi-verbal utterances, such as "Wow!" or "Really!" or even just

"Hmm," as appropriate.[7] Partners take turns speaking for two to three minutes while the other listens in this way. After even a simple exercise like this, we've seen couples come to a mutual understanding on issues that had remained unresolved for years. Why? Because no one actually listened at home, especially when things felt tense. It was the first time in a long time that either partner had really paid attention to what the other was saying.

If it's that simple, why don't people do it more often? To some extent, it's a matter of knowledge and skill. But even more important is attitude: do spouses actually *want* to listen to each other? It's not easy when one feels anxious or offended. And if their hearts are full of anger and contempt, it will show in their facial expression, body posture, or tone of voice, even if they superficially seem to be listening.

That's why in chapter 2 we spoke of the need for humility in marriage. Spouses tend to approach conflict in self-centered ways; each wants the other to listen but may not listen well himself or herself. Arguments escalate when one or both don't feel heard; they get angrier, then louder and more insistent—as if this would finally get the message across!

Listening, especially in the face of conflict and one's own emotional distress, embodies humility. Embodying the self-giving attitude of Jesus (e.g., Phil. 2:3-8), partners set aside the urge to make the other listen, and think relationally instead: *What I really want is for my spouse to listen to* me—*but I know he [or she] wants the same thing. Somebody has to listen. I'll set aside my need to talk, focus on him [or her], and trust that if I can show that I understand, he [or she] will calm down, and then I'll get a turn to say what I need to say.*

Again, teaching couples constructive communication is not about showing them the one and only right way to do things. Nor are these skills some kind of magic bullet to cure all marital ills. The goal is to create a more loving union in which both husband and wife feel accepted and understood by each other. When that attitude comes across clearly and consistently, much clumsiness in communication can readily be forgiven.

But even the most loving and accepting of spouses can be quick to take offense, setting off an emotional chain reaction. That's why it's important to encourage couples to learn to calm themselves down, and to teach them ways of communicating that help defuse the tension. Listening with full attention is still one of the best ways we know of to do that.

Pointing the couple again to the handout, explain the three basic principles below.[8] To make it easier, we've written the following sections as if *you* were a participant in a marriage communication workshop. Internalize the principles yourself, and begin putting them into practice, so that you can use your own words, experiences, and illustrations in teaching couples.

Focus Your Attention on Your Partner

When your spouse has something important to say, he or she usually wants your undivided attention. Sometimes that's not possible, as when supper is burning or a child is suddenly and violently ill. But few things communicate a lack of caring more than continuing to stare at a computer screen or television while your spouse is trying to get you to listen. It doesn't matter if you can actually repeat every word that was said if your body language says, "You're not as important to me as checking my Facebook or watching this program."

Show that you're interested in what your spouse has to say; turn away from distractions and toward him or her. Leaning in and making eye contact can also help, though sustained eye contact makes some people uncomfortable, for personal and cultural reasons. But even staring down at the floor can work, as long as he or she knows you're concentrating on what's being said.

The most important distraction to avoid is the one in your head. As you listen, it's natural to react to what your partner is saying. You may think that you're being accused of something you didn't do, or that he or she isn't getting the facts straight. And at that moment, the temptation is to stop listening and start planning your counterattack.

But consider the relational consequences. Even if you're right, your failure to listen will leave your partner feeling that it's no use trying to talk to you. If you notice yourself beginning to feel defensive, don't try to fight off the thoughts. That only feeds the distraction. Just *ignore* the defensive thoughts; let them go. Instead, *focus*—redouble your efforts to concentrate on your partner. If you can't and are feeling too overwhelmed, call for a time-out and try again later.

Try to Understand Both the Thoughts and the Feelings

When you have something important to say, you want the other person to "get it," which usually means acknowledging how you feel. Sometimes, you actually use feeling words: "When my boss said that, I was so mad I wanted to quit right then." That makes it easier for your partner to respond with understanding: "Wow—you were *furious!*" Other times, you may simply throw up your hands and shout, "Can you believe he said that?" But you would probably feel heard even if your partner did nothing more than shake his or her head and say, "Unbelievable!"

Now turn it around. Your partner needs the same kind of understanding from you. He or she may not use feeling words, so you may have to read the feeling from other cues such as facial expression and tone of voice. If you're not sure, imagine yourself in your partner's place: what would *you* be feeling in a similar situation? Don't worry about getting every emotional nuance just right; if your partner knows that you're *trying* to understand, that will feel supportive.

Of course, it's one thing to listen to how your partner feels about his or her boss; it's another to listen to how your partner feels about *you*. It's natural to start feeling defensive. But if your marriage is to succeed, both of you will have to make space for each other's feelings. Focus on *understanding* your partner's thoughts and feelings without trying to change them. Remember that you don't have to *agree*, so avoid the itch to criticize or pass judgment. Slow yourself down enough to listen carefully even to things you don't like hearing. As the authors of one relationship book have put it: "You are not truly listening unless you are prepared to be changed by what you hear."[9]

Show That You Understand

Here's where the two previous guidelines come together. You can focus on your partner, trying to understand the thoughts and feelings expressed, but he or she won't feel heard if you don't somehow *show* that you get it. Just saying "I understand" may not be enough by itself, especially if said with impatience. That behavior sends an un-helpful message: "OK, OK, can you stop talking now so I can say what *I* want to say?"

The classic way to show you understand is some form of restating what you hear: use a mixture of your partner's words and yours to say back what you heard. Using *his or her* words shows you've heard what was actually said; using *your* words shows you're taking it in and processing it personally. But generally, anything that shows you're tuned in and paying attention is fine (as in the response "Unbelievable!" earlier). The goal is for your partner to feel heard, and you'll know you've hit the mark when he or she keeps talking, nods, or says something like "Right!" or "Exactly!"

Thus, if your partner says, "Every time we go out to eat, it's Italian food. I'm sick of it," a simple response would be, "You're sick to death of Italian." That's a start. If you've been listening for both the thoughts and the feelings, as discussed above, you can take the empathy one step further by saying something that mirrors the underly-ing feeling: "A change would be nice!" What *wouldn't* work is, "Well, that's because you always leave it up to *me* to decide! Why don't *you* pick the restaurant for a change?" That kind of defensiveness makes it all about you, and will only escalate the tension.

This kind of paraphrasing helps slow down the process so you can focus on un-derstanding your partner. We've seen it over and over: when spouses take the time to listen, some problems, which were based on private misinterpretations of each other's behaviors, simply vanish. The reaction is, "Is *that* what you were thinking? I had no idea. I get it now."

In addition, saying something that helps your partner know that you understand his or her emotional state helps him or her feel loved and accepted. This lays the foundation for more constructive conversations, in which the two of you go back and forth, taking turns, listening in ways that help each of you feel understood, and speaking in ways that make it easier for each of you to listen nondefensively and well.

Speak in a Way That Makes It Easier to Listen

This is the flip side of the communication coin, the other skill in which you will coach couples. Even potentially difficult conversations can go well when both partners are committed to listening patiently and empathically, and to speaking with compassion for the other.

How we speak matters to God and to our relationships: "A gentle answer turns away wrath, / but a harsh word stirs up anger" (Prov. 15:1). We've seen the verse in James about the importance of listening. But the apostle also has something to say about the way we use words: "The tongue is a small part of the body, but it makes great boasts. Consider what a great forest is set on fire by a small spark. The tongue also is a fire, a world of evil among the parts of the body. It corrupts the whole body, sets the whole course of one's life on fire, and is itself set on fire by hell" (James 3:5-6). Could he say it any more strongly? The tongue is a fire; extending the metaphor, we think of people in relationships as surrounded by emotional tinder. All it takes is a few poorly chosen words to set feelings of offense and resentment ablaze, with far-reaching consequences.

Help couples think more relationally. Lashing out at someone may make them feel better for a few moments. It might even be justified. But what will it do to their marriage? Teach couples to value what's best for the relationship, not just the individuals—and that includes being wise with their words rather than popping off the first angry thing that comes to mind.

Thus, if the first principle is to listen in a way that helps one's partner to feel heard, the second is to speak in a way that makes it easier for one's partner to listen. This isn't about simply "getting one's feelings out." Careless words send a hurtful message: "Getting something off my chest is more important to me than you or our relationship." That triggers defensiveness and makes it far less likely that the speaker will be heard. And unfortunately, the speaker, in turn, is apt to blame the listener for being stubborn, stupid, or spiteful.

The alternative is to think relationally, to recognize that communication is always a two-way street. Both people have to bring something positive to the process. The listener brings nondefensive attentiveness and the desire to understand. Correspondingly, the speaker who thinks relationally should choose words that help the listener keep that nondefensive focus.

Help couples understand the speaker's responsibility to make a constructive contribution to marital communication, and then teach them the six specific principles below. Again, we've written the remainder of this chapter as if you were a participant in a marriage workshop.

Give Your Partner the Benefit of the Doubt

Here's a reminder: you're marrying someone who you generally love and admire, not someone stupid and mean. Right? But when you're upset or confused, it's easy to forget all that and to silently malign your partner's character. If that's what you're thinking, something negative is bound to creep into your body language or tone of voice.

Let's be honest. When you're upset with someone, that person feels like your enemy, and part of you wants to defend yourself or even get back at him or her. It's natural, but those who follow Christ must find another way, pursuing peace and striving for the good (Rom. 12:17-21). So ask yourself: do you really *want* to work things out, to build a stronger relationship, or just to push your partner away with your words?

Even in the best of marriages, people sometimes treat each other poorly. But we often make quick, emotionally driven judgments based on misinformation or misunderstanding. You may be absolutely right to be offended—but you could also be wrong. So consciously and deliberately give your partner the benefit of the doubt. Remind yourself that he or she is not an evil person to be attacked, or an idiot to be talked down to, or a child to be reprimanded. It's better for the relationship if you approach your partner with a more generous attitude.

Here are some action points that will help you embody that commitment.

Lead with the Positive

As a rule, since most of us respond defensively to criticism, an intentionally positive beginning can help keep the conversation from getting derailed at the start. For example, what if your spouse suddenly said to you, "We spend too much time with your family"? How would you feel? What would you say? Now imagine if the same conversation began, "I think we get along well with your family, and that's important to me. At the same time, I sometimes wish there was more time for *us* on vacations and holidays." Saying it this way does a number of things, including reminding each other of the positive things you value and appreciate. This makes for a softer "start-up"—which is a good predictor of how well it will go from there.[10]

Avoid Blaming and Name Calling

The basic idea is to avoid saying things in a way that will make your partner unnecessarily defensive. Many things you say can *feel* like an attack, whether you mean it that way or not. Your partner can hear, "It's all your fault" or "Everything would be fine if it weren't for you," even if you don't use those words. You can't control how he or she will respond, but you *can* take responsibility for getting your message across with less anger and spite.

When you're angry, you don't care much about *how* you say something; you just say it! That's despite the fact that Jesus portrays personal verbal attacks as no better than murder in God's eyes (Matt. 5:21-22). *You* probably don't enjoy being insulted or being told you did something wrong, even if it's true. Neither does your partner. So if you want him or her to actually hear what you have to say, edit out the negativity, the blaming, and the personal insults. You'll have to slow yourself down to do it. But that's the point.

For example, let's say the wife is on the neat side, and the husband isn't. To blurt out, "Must you always be so messy?" is an assault on his character, even if she doesn't call him a slob, because that global word *always*—said or implied—has a hidden sting. Or let's say she's freer with money than her husband would like. Shouting, "You bought what? You're going to spend us into the poorhouse!" will get him nowhere. She will react defensively, the conversation will stall, and they'll be no closer to a solution. So what's the alternative?

Speak Mostly about Your Own Thoughts and Feelings

Again, here's the wife who likes a tidy house, married to a man who tends to leave his dirty clothes lying about and crusty dishes piled up in the sink. Fed up, she explodes: "Why can't you clean up after yourself? I'm not your mother!" He's mystified. *I know you're not my mother*, he thinks, wondering why she would say something so obvious. But he keeps his mouth shut, and moments later, she storms out of the room, convinced once again that she's married to a man who just doesn't get it.

If she wants him to understand what she's feeling, she would do better to give him the benefit of the doubt. Instead of reading his mind ("I'm not your mother!"), she can tell him what's going on inside of her: "When you leave your dirty dishes piled up like that, I think you're expecting me to clean up after you, and I resent it."

This is an example of what are commonly known as "I-messages" or "I-statements."[11] Sadly, some people oversimplify the idea into a mechanical rule: "Begin every sentence with the words, 'I feel . . .' Never use the word *you*." Then they tie themselves into verbal knots, hoping that some relational magic will happen if they just use the right pronouns.

But that's not really the point. Here's the difference between the wife's two statements. In the first, she's obviously angry, and even though she doesn't say it directly, she makes the husband responsible for the way she feels. At least, that's how he'll take it.

Now contrast that with the second statement. She does in fact use the word *you*. But she does so to describe his *behavior* (leaving his dishes in the sink). When she speaks of his expectations of her (that she's supposed to clean up), she takes ownership of the fact that this is how she's interpreting his behavior ("I think"). None of this guarantees that he won't be defensive. But that second statement does a much better job of leaving the door open for a conversation about what his behavior *does* mean—provided that both are willing to listen!

Thus, being more careful about how you use the pronoun *you* can be helpful, since it often triggers defensiveness. But the more important and positive point is to stick to speaking about what you know—*your* thoughts, feelings, wishes, and opinions—instead of what's inside the other person. That's why I-statements are usually more effective. When you do say something about the other, try to keep it to simple descriptions of his or her *observable* behavior. That way, you help the person understand how his or her behavior has affected you. And in so doing, you're giving him or her the benefit of the doubt that he or she will want to do something about it.

Focus on the Present

When we try to tell our partners how they have hurt us in the present, it's tempting to drag in all the ways they've hurt us in the past. If you've ever had that done to you, you know how defensive it can make you feel, as if your partner were saying, "That's what makes you such a horrible person." That's why it's better to focus on the here and now. Avoid dredging up the past; it will only hamper you from making a positive connection with your spouse today.

For example, imagine your spouse saying to you, "We need to talk about last week, when you forgot to take care of the bills." Or worse, " . . . when you forgot *again*." Wouldn't your initial response be defensive? Here's how it might sound instead with a present focus and an eye toward a desirable future: "We need to talk about paying the bills. I want to discuss how we can come up with a plan that will make sure they get paid." That won't take away all the defensiveness. But by reducing the sense of blame, that statement does a better job of pulling the conversation forward, toward a resolution that you can work on together.

Make Room for Your Partner to Respond

Have you ever felt like someone was "dumping" on you? The person was distressed; emotions were running high. He or she poured out a litany of complaints, one after the other, hardly pausing to take a breath. How long was it before you became overwhelmed and weren't really listening anymore? A few minutes? A few seconds?

Good communication is a two-way street. The first partner speaks, being as constructive as possible, while the second listens attentively; then the second partner responds while the first listens attentively. Back and forth it goes, until hopefully both feel heard and understood.

Your responsibility as the speaker is to grease the wheels for that kind of back-and-forth conversation by making it easier for your partner to hear what you have to say. But he or she won't be able to do that if you overwhelm him or her with words, making it difficult to take it all in or to get a word in edgewise.

So here's the final principle: make room for your partner to listen and to respond. Concretely, that means pausing regularly and often so that your partner can say back to you what he or she heard. It's simple: if you want to be heard, you have to make space for the other person to practice listening.

Learn ways to stay calm when things get difficult; listen in a way that helps your partner feel heard; speak in a way that makes it easier to listen. These are the basic skills of constructive communication, of communicating in a way that helps to build a successful marriage. Doing these things will help you avoid unnecessary misunderstandings.

C h a p t e r
F i v e

Facing Conflict Together as a Couple

Early in my (Jim's) relationship, I saw my wife's gift for organization as complementing my flexibility and spontaneity. I appreciated her ability to get things done and to live a structured and ordered life. I often benefited from her ability to manage and organize. But shortly after getting married, when we had to live, work, and plan together, this difference became a source of significant conflict. My once endearing qualities of "game day" decision making and keeping options open collided with her need for planned predictability.

All couples will discover the differences between them; that's normal and expected. The question is how they will respond when they do. In the previous chapter, we focused on three skills of constructive communication:

1. calming down before having or continuing difficult discussions;

2. listening in a way that helps one's partner feel heard;

3. speaking in a way that makes it easier to listen.

The hope is that by coaching couples in these skills, you will be helping them prevent unnecessary conflicts over their differences.

Before they marry, however, couples often have idealized views of their partners. They may minimize the differences in their personalities and values, preferring to focus more energy on common interests and passions. For these reasons, premarital couples may not have struggled through a major disagreement yet. In time, their life together will erode overly positive views, and some couples, disillusioned, will see their relationship in new and negative ways.

That's why we've intentionally designed the Conversation Jumpstarter to gently undermine any such nearsighted idealization. Nudging couples outside their comfort zone raises the tension just enough for them to take learning constructive communication more seriously. Your job, as we've said, is to provide a safe and interactive environment in which the couple can develop their skill at discussing actual concerns. The greater their success during the premarital process, the stronger their sense of unity will be going into the marriage.

By cutting down on misunderstanding, good communication can help prevent unnecessary disagreements. But constructive communication won't magically eliminate all conflict from a marriage. Even when partners have appropriately expressed their thoughts and feelings, even when they have successfully listened to each other, they can still be discontent or perplexed. Or they may have reached a practical impasse: a decision needs to be made, and they've heard and understood each other's point of view, but they still disagree. What then?

In this chapter we will present important concepts that you can use to guide a couple in both strengthening their relationship against conflict as well as making decisions when spouses have conflicting needs. Our goal is not to have you solve a couple's disagreements for them, but rather to provide you with practices that you can teach couples to follow. In so doing, you will be preparing them for future success in handling what otherwise might have divided them.

Be Proactive Instead of Reactive

Engaged couples are no strangers to marital conflict. Often, one or both partners will have suffered the divorce of their own parents. They understand the importance of being proactive. Becoming more constructive in their communication is one way to do this, as is discussing how to strengthen their relationship against conflict in the first place. This is the conversation we introduced in chapter 3 as "option 2" for the third session. In this section, we will describe two proactive strategies that you can discuss with the couple.

Build More Positive Interaction into the Marriage

In chapter 4, we discussed the importance of "leading with the positive" when speaking. The bigger picture is that successful couples simply have more positive interaction than negative—much more. Even when dealing with difficult issues, these couples exhibit *five times* as many positive behaviors that communicate interest, care, humor, and warmth.[1] Other couples who are less able to regulate their negativity respond to each other with criticism, defensiveness, and contempt, behaviors that up the ante and lead to stonewalling or shutting each other out emotionally.[2]

Over time, the effect of this negativity puts the partners at greater risk for loneliness, disengagement, and even divorce. Moreover, negative emotions have the power to constrict one's thinking and attention. Expecting the worst, couples get caught in spirals of negative thought, entering conflict situations with a narrow view of the problem. By contrast, in positive emotional states, partners are more likely to see creative problem-solving options.[3]

This is not about "the power of positive thinking," but of positive *doing*. You probably know couples who look back longingly at their courtship and honeymoon, and wonder, *We used to have so much fun together. We used to laugh all the time and enjoy being together. What happened?* The sad fact is once we actually marry, it's too easy to get wrapped up in daily routines and to begin to take the relationship itself for granted.

Use the handout in appendix E, entitled "Making Our Marriage Stronger," to create a warm and life-giving conversation. Depending on the amount of time you have, you can either walk through the handout with the couple, explaining the importance of positivity, or assign it as homework and discuss it with them the next time. Have each partner tell the other what he or she already does that communicates interest, caring thoughtfulness, appreciation, concern, acceptance, and humor.[4] Then have the couple discuss concrete ways that they can preserve and build on these elements of their relationship after the wedding.

Here are two things to remember if you coach the conversation. First, this is not the time for them to complain about mutual failures, but rather to notice and build on successes. Focus on the positive. What do they already do that they want to keep doing, or even do more of once they're married? Second, help them to be as concrete as possible. It's not enough for them to say, "We love to laugh together, and don't want to lose that." Have them say, specifically, what they will do to keep laughter in their marriage. If you can't envision what they're saying as a behavior that occurs in a particular time and place, coach them to be more specific and to use their handout to write down a plan.

Recognize and Stop "the Dance"

The second proactive strategy begins with helping couples to recognize the typical "dance"—the repeating and mutually reinforcing pattern of hurtful steps—they fall into when approaching conflict. Over time, couples develop predictable patterns that become more evident when negative emotions hold sway, and couples default to a more reactive mode. The more intense and negative the emotion, the more rigid partners become in the stances they take. Some partners have an *approach* style of conflict, while others tend to *avoid* conflict at all costs. Most couples settle into a pattern that is defined by some combination of both, but either can produce a vicious cycle that feeds on negative emotion.

In the *approach/approach* dance, both partners fight with a "winner take all" mentality that makes the relationship feel less safe and discourages partners from depending on each other. *Avoid/avoid* couples shun talking about key differences in their relationship, living increasingly separate lives because they fear rocking the boat. Finally, *approach/avoid* couples, where partners take opposite positions, may fall into a repetitive pattern of one pursuing while the other withdraws.[5]

In a difficult argument, partners may handle their emotions according to the conflict styles described above. The partner with an approaching style, feeling an urgent need for resolution, pushes for a response. His or her anxiety, however, can drive the other partner farther away, which in turn fuels the first partner's original need for reassurance. As a result, the approaching partner may feel an increasing mix of fear, hurt, and alarm. These emotions may be difficult to communicate, especially if the predominant emotion is anger or frustration.

By contrast, partners who tend to avoid may feel like running away from urgent concerns. They keep their emotions under tight control or block them entirely, leaving them less in tune with themselves and more likely to miss their own or their partners' emotional signals. But emotions are an important source of information and motivation; the expressions of affection, concern, and love rely on emotional communication. Shutting them down, therefore, is problematic for the health of the marriage.

Some partners resist discussing their emotions because they don't trust them. Often, this is because they've been hurt when they opened themselves emotionally in the past. Such responses are understandable, but unfortunately they seldom lead partners to what they need most in moments of conflict and uncertainty. The absence of vulnerability in a relationship undermines the trust partners count on in marriage.

Watch and notice: what do partners do when things get tense? How do they respond to each other? Do they pursue, demanding attention and connection? Or do they withdraw, get quiet, or shut down? The patterns we've described are like an automatic and unhelpful dance of escalating negativity. Couples who are able to notice when the dance is beginning anew are also better able to warn each other and step out of the pattern, possibly even calling for a break (see chapter 4). In so doing, they can sometimes head off trouble before it gets too hard to handle.

Tracey and Patrick, for example, were arguing about their work schedules and social calendar when Patrick felt the tension rising in his chest. He picked up his smartphone and, following his usual pattern, immersed himself in e-mail as a way to avoid a more heated argument. Then he stopped, turned to Tracey, and said haltingly, "This is bothering me a lot and I'm about ready to check out. I don't want to do this. Can we take a break? I think I could do this better in an hour." Tracey, for her part, suddenly realized how she was pushing Patrick in a way that was making him anxious and defensive. She calmed herself and thanked him for letting her know about his frustration, and they agreed to try talking again in a little while.

This conversation can be particularly valuable if you've already noticed the couple's typical dance. Explain to them the *approach* and *avoid* styles of conflict. Which one do they think they are, and why? Ask for examples of what they actually do in the face of conflict, and coach them to describe their own behavior only. Explain the different dances—approach/approach, avoid/avoid, and approach/avoid—and have them think back on previous disagreements. Can they see the steps of the dance, and how the dance may have escalated? Add your own observations, if any, and be sure to frame them in purely descriptive, nonblaming words.

Watch their reactions during the conversation. Don't push the point with those who still seem doubtful. Instead, simply invite them to keep thinking about the idea in a proactive way: "If it still doesn't make sense to you, that's OK. Just start paying attention to anything that you typically do that would let you know that the dance is starting, and what you could do or say differently that would help both of you avoid getting into a fight."

But if they seem open to it, help them make a proactive plan for the future. Think back to the story of Tracey and Patrick above. What would be the concrete, observable signs that the dance is beginning? How could they warn each other in a way that would encourage a positive response? The point is for them to come up with one or two statements that would function as mutually agreed upon signals to stop, calm down, and use constructive communication.

For example, an approach-oriented spouse might say, "This is really important to me, but I don't want to come on too strong." A spouse who leans toward avoidance might say, "This whole thing is freaking me out and it's really hard for me to think straight." And for couples with a good sense of humor, it could be as simple as either of them saying, "Uh oh—I think I feel like dancing." There's no one right way to say it; each couple should come up with its own. Coach them through a constructive conversation in which each one could agree, "Yes, if you said that to me, it would help me step back, slow down, or get some perspective." Will it always work? There are no guarantees. But it helps to have some prearranged reminder of their mutual commitment to recognize and stop the negative dance, for the sake of their unity as a couple.

Making Decisions When Needs Conflict

"Option 3" for the third session works best when there are practical decisions to be made but the partners disagree. The more intangible aspects of the relationship, such as deeper issues of trust, acceptance, and sexual desire, are not concrete decisions that lend themselves well to the kind of process described below. If you think the couple is stuck on these kinds of fundamental issues, it may be best to refer them to therapy.

In general, navigating conflict always begins with constructive communication. But couples will also benefit from having an organizing structure and shared strategy for working out specific differences. In this section we give you five simple steps for guiding couples through situations in which they need to decide on a course of action but their needs and preferences conflict.

In its most popular form, the strategy can be traced back to the "no-lose" method of conflict resolution that psychologist Thomas Gordon taught to parents in the 1960s.[6] Today, the same basic principles can be found in a variety of curricula, including empirically supported approaches to relationship enhancement and marital therapy.[7] Gordon's contribution was to frame the conflict between two people in terms of their competing needs, and no-lose conflict resolution is a process whereby the two parties work together to come up with a creative solution in which the needs of both are met.

Because the terms "conflict resolution" and "problem solving" have such broad implications, we prefer in this book to speak more narrowly of a five-step process of "decision making," to help you and your couples remember when the method would be appropriate. Give the couple the handout from appendix F, entitled "Making Decisions When Our Needs Conflict." For their first time learning the method, we recommend that you *not* give it to them as homework but rather coach them through the steps in person.

Step 1. Define the Specific Disagreement to Be Discussed

Arguments sometimes grow and take on a life of their own because partners get so wrapped up in proving their point or winning the fight that they don't notice the argument spinning off onto one tangent after another. A couple will not be able to successfully navigate their way through a disagreement unless they focus on one issue at a time and agree what that issue is. Help them define the disagreement by filling in the spaces on the handout. First, what is the practical decision that needs to be made? In chapter 3, we suggested the examples of how they will keep bank accounts or where they will spend their first Christmas. Other examples include who to invite to the wedding or how much time they will spend with their individual friends after they're married. Again, it works best to start with some impasse that's already come up in previous conversations.

Next, have them fill in the lines below where they've described the decision. What does she want? What's the decision she'd like him to accept? What does he want? For what alternative decision does he want to argue? Up to this point, the disagreement may not have been defined that explicitly because one partner hasn't really said what he or she wants, as when the husband simply shoots down every suggestion his wife makes, without offering any suggestions of his own.

As coach, you may need to help one partner—or even both partners—identify and voice the result he or she really wants. Sometimes, the so-called magic wand may point the conversation in the right direction: "If you could wave a magic wand over the situation and have any outcome you want, what would it be?"

Step 2. Redefine the Conflict in Terms of Needs

This is a crucial step for the unity of the relationship, and often the most difficult. Step 1 only makes the disagreement clear and heightens the adversarial expectation: we can't have it both ways, so who's going to win? But the point of Gordon's method and message is that if conflicts are defined in adversarial terms, nobody really wins because the *relationship* loses. Why? Behind each proposed solution is usually some legitimate—and often unspoken or unrecognized—need. And that means the one who loses the contest gets the message "My needs aren't important in this marriage." When that happens, the marriage is the real loser.

In step 2, therefore, you must help the couple redefine what they wrote in step 1 in terms of an underlying need—or perhaps more than one need. Take the bank accounts example. During their Jumpstarter discussion of money, it becomes clear that Sue wants to pool all their income as a couple and keep it in jointly owned and accessed accounts. Bill, however, is equally adamant about having separate accounts. What to do?

This is one reason we've built such an emphasis on family-of-origin experiences into the CJ. The couple's disagreement about how to handle their money isn't an intellectual discussion about proper economic policy. It comes freighted with emotions that have been shaped by previous experience.

Sue came from a home in which her parents lived largely parallel and separate lives, keeping their money to themselves and spending it on a whim without consulting each other. They eventually divorced. To her, how they keep money is a symbol of togetherness. Bill, by contrast, came from a family in which all the household money was kept in a single account. Mom paid the bills; Dad was addicted to online gambling. More than once, the mortgage payment bounced because Dad had emptied out the account to support his habit. Therefore, to Bill money is a potent symbol of trustworthiness and security.

As their coach, use the handout to help the couple dig beneath the surface, to find the need that lies beneath the outcome they're fighting for. For example, you might say, "Sue, you want joint accounts, and Bill, you want individual accounts. I know it may sound strange, but we want to try to find a solution that's going to work for both of you. But before we do that, we need to figure something else out first. Sue, it seems as if keeping the money in one account isn't just a mild preference—it's *important* to you. Bill, same thing—having individual accounts is *important* to you. The question is *why*.

"Look at the handout. Sue, I want you to complete this sentence: 'I want to have a joint account because I need to know or I need to feel _____.' Bill, for you, it would be: 'I want separate accounts because I need to know or I need to feel _____.' How would you both fill in those blanks? Think about it for a moment and write it down." Sue, for example, might fill in the blank by writing, "I need to feel like we're really a *couple*, not just two individuals living in the same house." Bill might write: "I need to know that we're never going to find ourselves on the street." As coach, you might gently prod Bill to go even deeper, to "I need to feel safe." This is again a good place to help them practice constructive communication so that they both express their needs appropriately and listen to each other compassionately.

The point of step 2 is to take what might seem like an all-or-nothing, win-lose decision and reframe it as a conflict of legitimate needs. Sue may want to advocate for a joint account, but not at the expense of Bill's feeling of safety. Bill may want to insist on separate accounts, but not if it means Sue thinking he's not committed to the marriage.

Not every decision, of course, carries that much emotional baggage. "What do you feel like eating tonight?" is the kind of decision that usually jumps straight to the process of brainstorming without passing through a discussion of needs. You and the couple will know the difference by the intensity with which partners defend their preferred solutions.

Step 3. Brainstorm Possible Alternatives

Once you have clearly identified a specific disagreement to discuss, and have reframed it in terms of underlying needs, you are ready to begin generating possible solutions. Tell the couple as they begin that this process will only work if they're willing to set aside their desire to lobby for their preferred solution; get them to acknowledge and agree to this condition.

Then take out a single piece of paper. The partners are to take turns suggesting possible solutions, saying and then writing down whatever comes to mind. At this stage, no idea, no matter how outlandish it might seem, is to be ruled out.

As coach, your job is to keep the atmosphere playful. Laughter is good! Remember what we said earlier: negative emotions can strangle the imagination. There may be a wonderfully creative solution to a couple's situation, but when they're in the grip of negativity neither partner will see it. Help them keep the ideas coming. If the process seems to bog down, throw in a humorous suggestion of your own. But avoid inserting or advocating for your own ideas of what they should do; the best-case scenario is for them to generate and embrace their own solution.

Brainstorming gives them the freedom to be more playful with an issue that had previously been divisive and hurtful. Here, for example, is part of Sue and Bill's list:

1. Put all of our money in a joint account.

2. Put all of our money in separate accounts.

3. Put some money in a joint account and some in separate accounts.

4. Stuff everything under the mattress.

5. Spend it all as soon as it comes in.

6. Quit our jobs, buy a farm, grow our own food, and become self-sufficient.

Idea number six comes from Bill. He says it jokingly at first, and they have a good laugh. But then he also realizes that part of him longs for some alternative to city life and the forty-hour workweek. It leads to a brief discussion of his dreams, a conversation that helps Sue understand her fiancé a little better and brings them closer. That's one potential benefit of brainstorming. Just remember: at this step, the goal is to generate ideas, not to evaluate them.

Step 4. Agree on One Alternative and Make a Plan

Once they have their list, the next step is deciding on one alternative to try. They can begin by crossing off any ideas that they agree were suggested just for fun. For the others, help them keep step 2 in mind: which idea offers the best shot at meeting the needs of both partners?

Bill and Sue, for example, quickly and laughingly cross alternatives four and five off the list. Sue then looks at Bill, and with some hesitation crosses off number one, saying, "Having our money together in a shared account is still really important to me, but I don't want to do that if it makes you feel unsafe." Bill responds by crossing off number two: "Thanks. And I don't want to do anything that leaves you feeling like I'm not in this marriage 100 percent."

They both agree that number three seems like the best option. That solution may have seemed painfully obvious to you from the beginning, so much so that you had to bite your tongue to keep from suggesting it yourself! What's important, however, is that they come to this decision with a spirit of conscious collaboration rather than hasty compromise. If they had made that decision without an understanding of their underlying needs, one or both would have felt taken advantage of, like they had given up something important just to appease an unreasonable partner. This way, Bill and Sue each have more of a mutual stake in doing what's best for the relationship.

Next, they need a clear and unambiguous plan for putting the decision into place. Will they have joint checking *and* savings accounts? Individual accounts for both of them, or just Bill? How much money goes into each kind of account? Do they want to make an agreement about how much one person can spend out of the joint account without consulting the other?

Depending on the complexity of the decisions being made, it may help to put the plan in writing. What are the steps? Who is responsible to do what, and when? Making a clear timetable with assigned responsibilities will help avoid misunderstanding.

Step 5. Schedule a Progress Review

Any agreement should be treated as a pilot test at first. Help the couple set a time to review whether the solution is working for each of them and for their relationship. Bill and Sue, for example, might agree to sit down six months after the wedding to see if the decision they made needs to be modified on the basis of met and unmet needs.

A scheduled progress review helps them avoid the resentment of having to live too long with a solution that isn't working. For some decisions, like Bill and Sue's, a six-month trial period may seem reasonable. In other cases, the couple may need to check back with each other in a week or a month.

Encourage them to return to the needs discussion and brainstorming process if they find that the decision isn't working out for one or both of them. If they stay the course with constructive communication and a collaborative process for making decisions, then even ineffective solutions can help them understand the problem and each other better. They can learn from what didn't work and use the knowledge to strengthen their relationship.

In this chapter, we've presented some options you can insert into the latter stages of the premarital preparation process to help couples face conflicts in a way that builds their unity instead of tearing it down. But you can also look for opportunities anywhere in the process to explore how they respond to each other's attempts to repair rifts in the relationship. We'll discuss that in the next chapter, as we review in greater detail what it means to be their coach.

C h a p t e r
S i x

Coaching the
Conversations

Throughout this book, we've intentionally used the language of "coaching" rather than "counseling" couples. Having outlined the entire Jumpstarter process (chapter 3) and the skills through which you will guide couples (chapters 4 and 5), it's time for us to say more about the coaching role itself.

I (Cameron) remember my short stint coaching my son's fourth-grade city basketball team, a ragtag bunch of kids culled from different schools in the community. Some had never touched a basketball before, while others were already highly skilled. My job was to teach them the fundamentals—dribbling, passing, and shooting—while trying to get them to play together as a team. Not exactly being a gym rat myself, I had to work at my own shooting form and other skills before I had anything to teach them.

At game time, *they* were the ones on the court, not me. They had to make the moment-to-moment decisions about how and when to use what they'd learned. They had to generalize their use of basic skills to different game situations and opponents, figuring out how to play as a team when facing a variety of unpredictable challenges. I could only watch from the sidelines, occasionally shouting instructions or calling a time-out when the play began to unravel. Between games, we'd go back to ball-handling drills.

And perhaps just as important, I tried to make it fun. I never berated or humiliated the kids, even when they dribbled the ball off their foot or passed it to someone who wasn't looking, hitting the unsuspecting boy squarely in the back. I wanted them to enjoy being with their teammates and to look forward to getting out on the court.

This, essentially, is what we're asking you to do with couples.

You are teaching them relationship fundamentals and putting them through practice drills. They learn by scrimmaging in your office while you actively give instructions, sometimes even stopping play for a reminder or a short practice drill. You do all this with the hope of building their skills as a team. They're the ones who are in the game; they need to internalize the skills well enough to be able to face whatever opponent life sends their way.

People generally seek counselors when they have a problem, with the expectation of receiving expert advice and even a solution. But marriage preparation is a little different. The focus is on prevention rather than correction, skill development rather than problem solving. It's like the old proverb "Give a man a fish and you feed him for a day. Teach a man to fish and you feed him for a lifetime."

In the flexible structure we've described, whatever counseling training you already have should serve you well. But try to stay in the role of coach rather than counselor. Even though some of the discussion will naturally bring up issues from their families of origin, your primary and time-limited task is not to resolve past hurts, but to encourage self-awareness and mutual understanding in the present in order to prepare couples for the future.

In this chapter, we'll describe what good coaching involves. The first section will address general principles, while the latter sections will make more specific recommendations about how to help couples respond to each other in relationship-building ways.

General Principles

Coaching is more active than advice giving. A good coach doesn't just tell players what to do, but he or she also demonstrates the desired skills and helps players actively practice them, giving immediate guidance and correction as needed. Coaching premarital couples is not inherently difficult work, but for it to succeed, you'll need to keep your proper role in mind at all times. Here, then, are four basic principles or directives that will help you be a more effective coach overall. The first three are relatively straightforward. The fourth requires greater skill from you, so we'll discuss it in much greater detail.

Model the Skills You're Coaching

Couples don't come to you as blank slates. They each have a history with each other as well as with their families and friends. Chances are, there was little if any explicit discussion of constructive ways to communicate in any of these relationships. In other words, you may be trying to teach couples skills that they've never seen modeled by anyone!

You will, of course, use words to describe the skills as a necessary first step. But often, what you say won't make much sense to the couple until they actually see the skills in action. "Don't do as I do, do as I say" is as poor a philosophy for marriage education as it is for the Christian life! If you don't show couples by your own behavior what the skills look like in practice, they may neither understand nor appreciate what you're teaching them. You don't have to be perfect at it. Just show that you value the skills enough to put them to personal use.

Pragmatically, it's also more difficult to show people how to do something you don't do relatively well yourself. As baseball great Yogi Berra reportedly said, "You've got to be very careful if you don't know where you are going, because you might not get there." (Then again, he's also famous for the line, "I really didn't say everything I said.") So if you want to help couples improve their relationship skills, then practice, practice, practice what you preach.

Emphasize Active Practice

Imagine a basketball coach teaching players to shoot free throws: "Here, stand like this, feet like so. Square your shoulders to the basket. Bend your knees." After five minutes of instruction, a player attempts the shot and misses. "No, no, not like that," the coach says, and another five-minute lesson follows. Then, as the player steps to the free-throw line for the second time, the coach has a sudden inspiration: "You know, that reminds me of a story. I remember when my dad taught me the importance of follow-through . . ."

It may be tempting to fall into sermons or mini-lectures. But when it comes to skills, people learn best by trying, failing, and trying again. Always look for ways to get couples to *do* something conversationally while you coach them. If the couple tells you a story about how a conversation went awry, don't just give verbal advice. Have them *show* you what went wrong, and actively redirect their behavior on the spot. Make your instructions as simple and to the point as possible. If you've already explained something to them, a brief reminder should suffice, such as, "Whoa! Speak for yourself."

Favor Good Outcomes over Perfect Process

Let's go back to the free-throw line for a minute. During a game, some players routinely clank one shot after another off the rim. Clearly, they need to go back and practice the fundamentals. But others are able to consistently sink the shot using some variation of the basics. What matters is getting the ball through the hoop. So while we believe there are communication "fundamentals," success doesn't mean slavish adherence to the rules.

For example, how much does it matter if someone doesn't form a perfect "I-statement" or doesn't say it the way you think he or she should? What if a person's listening seems a little off the mark? Watch the reactions. Does the other partner relax, or get tenser? Maintain eye contact, or look away? Give signs of being heard, or of being misunderstood? If what the person is doing is working, if it seems to be creating a positive connection, don't stymie the process by inserting a criticism. Encourage the part you liked, and leave the correction for later, if at all.

Interrupt and Redirect as Necessary

Some couples will understand right away what you're teaching them and need little direction. Others will require firmer guidance. When conversations turn in unproductive or even hurtful directions, you may need to step in, halt the process, and redirect them into something more constructive. There are two basic situations in which you may need to do this.

As suggested in chapter 1, the first is when you need to stay on task because of time constraints. You have only so many hours with a couple before they marry, and that time should be considered precious. It's fine, for example, to have a few minutes to chitchat and connect at the beginning of sessions. But letting it go on too long can sometimes be a way of avoiding the work that needs to be done.

During a conversation, one partner may go on and on for a variety of reasons, in a way that doesn't seem constructive. For example, when answering a question, someone may spin off into a story that's only marginally related at best. Don't encourage the tangent. If things get too chatty, show that you're listening and interested, and then gently but firmly bring the conversation back: "That *does* sound like an interesting book! I may need to check that out. Martha, let's go back to something you said a couple of minutes ago."

Or a person may continue speaking because he or she is riding a tidal wave of emotional energy (positive or negative). The individual is not pausing for turn taking, and the other partner may feel lost or overwhelmed. In such cases, you may actually have to interrupt the person in order to redirect the conversation. This is a more delicate skill to master, so go slowly at first. The important thing to remember is that whatever you do, the goal is still for the person to feel heard and understood. That's the basis for his or her accepting your redirection gracefully.

How do you interrupt without offending the other person? It may sound paradoxical, but it begins with becoming more active and energetic in your *listening* responses. Don't just sit quietly nodding. Lean in; nod more vigorously; respond to his or her words with short comments of your own (e.g., "Wow!" "Ouch!" "No kidding!" and so on). Overlap the person's speech with a brief comment that conveys empathy and understanding. This is crucial: redirecting too quickly or interrupting without empathy can amplify the emotion instead of containing it. When the speaker pauses, and has taken the interruption well, insert a question or comment that will get the process back on track. If the speaker doesn't pause, take the strategy one step further: overlap the talkative person with actual sentences, and then redirect.

Here's an example. The couple is discussing money. Franco, visibly upset, begins telling a story about how his parents fought over the finances. Don't wait for him to run out of steam. Begin overlapping him with longer utterances, from "Wow!" to "You hated that!" and eventually to, "There was chaos when Dad spent that much without discussing it with Mom first!" Bringing up your energy—with *empathy*—will help Franco calm down. Then you'll be able to redirect: "Franco, I'm wondering what that might mean for your relationship with Jennie. How do you want monetary decisions to be handled in your marriage?"[1]

The second situation is when you interrupt to stop negative behavior or break up bad habits. Over time, couples create relational ruts in their communication, falling automatically into stereotyped and unhelpful patterns that become more obvious when partners are feeling tense or distressed. This is why couples in marriage workshops frequently report breaking through an impasse when doing a communication exercise. At home, left to their own devices, they keep rolling down the same ruts over and over; but when they are forced to relate differently, they discover that the problem was with the process, not the person.

You want couples to practice constructive communication, not deepen their destructive ruts. If you see them doing something unhelpful, don't wait for the end of the conversation or even the end of the sentence; interrupt immediately and redirect. Simply say "Whoa!" or "Yikes!" or "Time-out!"—anything that gets their attention and stops the negative process. Then give a simple instruction to get the process back on track.

For example, Jennie is telling Franco that something he wrote in response to the CJ worries her, and Franco erupts defensively. Intervene *immediately*. "Whoa! Time-out, Franco. Jennie, finish what you're saying, and keep it short. Franco, listen and tell her what you heard." You may need to do this more than once. If Franco still can't calm down, give him the space to express to you what he's feeling, and coach him to do it in a way that doesn't blame Jennie. When he seems to feel understood, go back to the conversation between them and have them try again. If he still isn't able to stay calm and listen, suggest the possibility of working with a therapist. But whatever you do, make it your active responsibility to interrupt negative patterns of interaction and steer them into something more positive.

These four principles should give you a good sense of the coaching role overall. In the sections that follow, we'll give more specific pointers about coaching the couple in skills related to listening, speaking, and responding to each other's attempts to repair the relationship.

Coaching Couples to Listen with Attention and Empathy

One of your tasks as coach is to help couples learn to listen to each other with the kind of empathy that helps their partner feel heard. Usually, that means giving their full attention and feeding back the essence of what they're hearing and especially what the partner is feeling. But as we said above, you don't have to be rigid about the process if you're getting the right outcome. What constitutes good listening? To paraphrase Jesus, you shall know it by its fruit.

The signs are relatively easy to spot when the conversation is less tense. As mentioned in chapter 4, when the listener responds accurately, the speaker may nod and keep going, sometimes with a straighter path to what he or she wanted to say. When the listener is not only accurate but also empathic, the speaker may respond more energetically, with an emphatic "Right!" or "Exactly!" But when the listener misses the mark, the speaker may seem frustrated or even confused, with a facial expression that says, "Where did *that* come from?"

Sometimes the cues are subtler. In general, observe the speaker's body language and facial expression; listen to the tone of voice. When he or she first begins speaking, you will often see signs of distress. The person may seem tense and agitated: muscles are tight; the jaw is clenched; his or her voice is strained. Or the speaker may seem sullen and withdrawn: eyes are downcast; the body droops; his or her voice is barely audible.

When the partner's listening is on target, you should see and hear a change in the speaker. The agitated person begins to relax, coming across more softly and with less intensity. The withdrawn person seems to perk up: the voice gets stronger, and he or she may even make eye contact. These changes may not happen right away. But as long as the speaker is not becoming *more* agitated or withdrawn, you probably don't need to change what the listener is doing.

Here are two common situations in which you need to be active in coaching a listener. The first was already illustrated by the story of Jennie and Franco above: the person who is supposed to be listening fails to do so. Remember, the speaker is taking a risk by being vulnerable with his or her feelings, assuming that the other partner will listen. You have a responsibility to try to keep the conversational atmosphere safe. Don't hesitate. Interrupt the listener and give a quick reminder: "Hang on a second! Listen first."

In the second situation, the listener seems unable to listen because he or she is "flooding"—that is, feeling emotionally overwhelmed by what the speaker is saying. Here are some typical signs that people may be flooding:

- They close their eyes for a long time.

- They fold their arms across their chest.

- They go silent, with expressions of blankness, fear, anger, or sadness.

- They hold their breath.

- They display some anxious tic, like playing with their hair or bouncing their legs.[2]

When that happens, people will be nearly incapable of listening until the emotion subsides.

Turn your attention to the person who is flooding, and make an observation: "You seem to be experiencing some pretty strong emotions right now." If you don't get an outright denial, ask him or her to tell you what he or she is feeling, while you listen empathically. When the person is calmer, probe gently to see if he or she would be willing to try telling what he or she is feeling to the partner, while you coach. If not, consider taking a short break.

Some of the conversations in the premarital process will be more difficult than others, by design. It's natural for one or both partners to feel anxious; in most cases, you should be able to coach them through it. But if one or both partners flood repeatedly during your conversations, the couple would probably benefit more from seeing a marital therapist.

Coaching Couples to Notice and Express Their Feelings Clearly and without Blame

In chapter 4, we presented six principles to help couples speak in a way that would make it easier for their partners to listen. The skills described are not difficult to coach: you merely have to pay close attention to what the speaker is saying, notice when he or she is falling into negative behavior, and be ready to jump in and redirect as needed.

What may be trickier is getting people to put their feelings into words in the first place. Couples need to do this to be able to manage their emotional experience, especially when facing a disagreement or heated issue. The problem is that many find it difficult to do, fear the vulnerability it entails, or believe that emotions will get in the way of a calm, rational conversation. For these and other reasons, they try to deny, suppress, or block their emotions.

Quite simply, it doesn't work. Instead, the emotion gets expressed indirectly in the present, through body language or tone of voice, or later, in the form of aloofness or misplaced anger. Imagine what happens, for example, when a couple moves too quickly to compromising on some issue, and one of the partners still feels unfairly blamed. Ignoring the feeling of resentment doesn't remove it. Indeed, research has shown that trying to suppress negative emotions, especially under pressure, can actually make them worse.[3] The feelings don't go away—they just show up somewhere else.

To be clear, we are *not* suggesting that everything a couple says has to include an "I feel . . ." component. Some disagreements stem from misunderstandings that could be resolved with new information. I (Cameron) remember secretly resenting one of my students for always falling asleep during my lectures, until I discovered she had a chronic medical condition that required a drug that made her drowsy. I didn't need to send her an "I-statement" about my resentment; I needed a piece of information that I didn't have! But in the intimate relationship of marriage, how one partner feels frequently *is* the piece of information the other partner needs in order to connect on an empathic level. The importance of expressing the emotion clearly is directly proportional to the strength of the emotion itself.

There are two broad implications for you as their coach. First, helping couples express their feelings may begin with helping them notice and acknowledge their emotions. Let's say Luke and Laura are having a conversation about how they want to relate to their respective families as a couple. Luke thinks Laura's family is intrusive, and he bombards her with example after example of her mother's inappropriate behavior. Laura knows that her mother can be difficult, but loves and is deeply loyal to her.

Remember the distinction between *content* and *process* from chapter 1? You can see it in the verbal tennis match between Luke and Laura—they argue at the level of content. "Then, your mother said this." "No, she didn't." "Yes, Laura, she did." "Well, maybe she did, but that's not what she meant." Back and forth it goes, pushing the couple further and further apart, with no progress toward agreement.

The problem is that they're failing to connect at the emotional level—because they aren't acknowledging and expressing how they feel about what the other is saying. Think about it. If you were Laura, how would you feel about your husband-to-be criticizing your mother? Offended? Sad? Protective? If you were Luke, how would you feel about your bride-to-be taking her mother's side instead of yours? Hurt? Betrayed? If the conversation is in fact prompting such strong emotions, you will need to get them to communicate at that level.

You may first have to interrupt the tennis match: "OK, OK, time-out you two. Let's slow things down a little." Make an observation about the process: "This doesn't seem to be going anywhere. It's certainly not bringing you any closer to each other!" Then redirect: "I suspect you both have some pretty strong feelings about what the other person is saying. Laura, can you tell Luke how you feel about the things he said about your mom?" Coach her to express herself constructively, while simultaneously coaching Luke to listen as needed. When Laura agrees that Luke has understood her feelings, you can ask him to voice his emotions as well.

The second implication is that you may need to pay particular attention to how they label and express their emotions. Imagine, for example, that in response to your redirection, Laura turns to Luke and says, "I feel like you hate my mother." The problem with that statement is that it comes across as an accusatory bit of mind reading, and is almost certain to trigger defensiveness. Even if Luke is able to hear the pain in Laura's statement, his response may remain stuck at the content level: "Laura, I don't hate your mother." That only invites another turn on the "Yes, you do" and "No, I don't" merry-go-round.

When people clearly express their feelings, it usually takes the form "I feel X," where X names an actual emotion. But when someone inserts the word *that* or *like*, as Laura did—"I feel *that* X"—what you may be getting is an opinion or judgment. When that happens, you can reframe and then redirect: "So Laura, when Luke criticizes your mother like that, you think he hates her. Tell him how that makes you feel." Coach her to express her feeling in a simple nonblaming way, and help Luke listen.

Coaching Couples to Respond Positively to Repair Attempts

In marriage, it's inevitable: there are times when conflicts will escalate and tensions will rise. What happens then? In many couples, one or the other spouse will reach out in some way, will do something to try to bridge the gulf between them. It can be as simple and unsophisticated as putting on a contrite and sheepish grin.

In successful couples, the other spouse responds positively to such overtures, whereas in unsuccessful couples, partners may try repeatedly to heal the rift, but to no avail. John Gottman calls these relational overtures "repair attempts":

> This name refers to any statement or action—silly or otherwise—that prevents negativity from escalating out of control. . . . When a couple have a strong friend-

ship, they naturally become experts at sending each other repair attempts and at correctly reading those sent their way. But when couples are in negative override, even a repair statement as blunt as "Hey, I'm sorry" will have a low success rate. The success or failure of a couple's repair attempts is one of the primary factors in whether their marriage flourishes or flounders. And again, what determines the success of their repair attempts is the strength of their marital friendship.[4]

What Gottman calls "negative override" refers to a distressed couple's predisposition to interpret everything in negative and defensive terms. Persistent negativity in the relationship casts a pall over the marriage, and invitations to repair are rejected. However, in successful couples, there is a *positive* override instead. Because their marital friendship is strong, they naturally give each other the benefit of the doubt, and accept each other's attempts at repair.

Repair attempts come in all shapes and sizes. A partner might step back in the midst of a disagreement and talk about what was happening at a relationship level: "Hey, it feels like things are getting out of control. How about if we slow it down a little?" There may be attempts at humor, affection, compassion, apology, or some other means of soothing each other and reinforcing their sense of being a team.

But Gottman's point is not to say that better repair attempts make for better marriages. Rather, it's nearly the other way around: in more positive marriages, partners are more responsive to repair, regardless of how sophisticated the method. Where friendship abounds, even the goofiest attempt is usually met with acceptance and gratitude.

There are two implications of this for you as coach. First, think back to what we said in the last chapter about proactively building more positivity into the marriage. Even if you elect not to have that particular discussion with the couple as part of your preparation process, you can still look for ways to encourage positivity during your other conversations.

For example, you can notice the positive things they do, even when they're not disagreeing, and comment on them appreciatively: "Fred, I noticed that as you started talking you reached over and took Wilma's hand affectionately. That's great! Wilma, how did you feel when he did that?" Making observations like that will encourage them to value the positivity that already exists in the relationship and to be even more positive in the future.

Second, in tandem with the first strategy, you may want to have couples talk explicitly about repair, particularly when you notice either successful or unsuccessful attempts in their actual conversations. What did one person do to reach out, and how did the other person respond? Betty, for example, may spontaneously reach over to touch Barney's arm when he seems upset. But Barney pulls his arm away, and Betty looks defeated.

You can make an observation and start a discussion from there. Did they notice when it happened? What were they feeling? What other things do they do to try to reach out to each other, and how do they typically respond? Which behaviors succeed at communicating care and concern, and which don't? Again, the point is not necessarily to "improve" their repair strategies, but to make them more aware of when their partner is in fact reaching out. This primes them to respond with greater acceptance when repair attempts happen, building the positivity in their marriage and contributing to the positive override that makes the relationship stronger and more resilient.

Your role as a coach is an active one. You don't just tell couples about relationship skills; you show them what the skills look like, give them opportunities to practice, reinforce their successes, and redirect them when they get off track. When done well, the coaching process will create a bond between you and the couple that will lend depth and warmth to your role as the officiant at their wedding. We like to think of coaching as an organic expression of pastoral care. In the remaining chapters, we'll offering ideas and insights for coaching conversations around each of the six topics in the Jumpstarter.

Part Three

Conversation
Topics

C h a p t e r
S e v e n

Roles and
Responsibilities

From the moment they met, Veronica and Reggie were aware of the differences in their cultural backgrounds. However, it didn't take long for them to discover that those cultures shared one important thing in common: they were quite traditional in their expectations of the roles that husbands and wives should play in the home. Consequently, they both grew up with fathers who were the sole or primary "bread-winners" and had little to do with housekeeping chores or caring for the children. These latter tasks were clearly Mom's domain and responsibility. To the extent that their fathers did any work inside the house, such as cooking or cleaning, it was generally viewed as "helping" Mom. And to the extent that she earned any income, it was viewed as a supplement to Dad's wages, not as an independent career.

But Veronica and Reggie also found themselves growing up in America during a time of continuous cultural change. In principle, both of them vaguely wanted a marriage that was more egalitarian, even though neither of them had seen it modeled in their own families. Veronica had a part-time career and did most of the housework and child care. Reggie was a very involved father, and did more around the house than *his* dad ever did—but still far less than Veronica. So while Reggie felt like a pretty generous guy compared to his father, Veronica felt that he still wasn't pulling his fair share of the load compared to *her*.

Engaged couples seldom talk explicitly about the roles and responsibilities, routines and rituals that will come with forming a new household. Who's going to do what around the house once they get married? Who will work outside the home? Will that work be a career or just a way to earn some extra income? Not realizing that they may come with different expectations, the prospective spouses may take the answers to such questions for granted.

More pointedly, the question is not just "Who *will* do what?" but "Who *should* do what?" Many couples attach at least some sense of right and wrong to such matters.

They have values and preferences that are largely unacknowledged but strongly felt: husbands are *supposed* to do one thing, wives another. And doesn't everyone know that there's only one proper way to load a dishwasher?

The central issue is fairness. Some sociologists have argued that in every marriage there are actually two marriages, "his" and "hers," and that husbands benefit more from marriage than do their wives.[1] The perennial bone of contention has been the distribution of work and family responsibilities. Working women are still often expected to keep up with their traditional duties as wives and mothers, putting in a domestic "second shift" even after a long day at the office.[2]

We'll leave it to the sociologists and demographers to settle how deep and wide the "his versus hers" imbalances run in the nation as a whole. Pragmatically, however, we must recognize that this is a common cause of tension and resentment between spouses:

> With the advent of so many dual career marriages, the division of domestic responsibilities has become a major source of marital conflict. Changes in our cultural values have contributed greatly to the problem, because there is now almost unanimous agreement that both a husband and wife should share these responsibilities, particularly child care. But change in behavior has not kept pace with the change in values.[3]

The bride and groom's expectations may not be explicit. Neither of them is likely to be fully aware of all the "shoulds" they bring into the marriage. And none of this may matter much as long as both spouses have plenty of time and freedom to do as they please. But when they have to start working harder inside or outside the home—as when children are born—fairness can become a very real issue between them. The first section of the Conversation Jumpstarter seeks to give couples a head start on that discussion.

There's Work to Be Done!

Men and housework. For many women, the combination is a rich, if somewhat snarky, source of humor. Here's our retelling of one joke, origin unknown, that we've seen in various versions around the Internet: A laundry-challenged husband one day decided to be helpful and wash his own stinky sweatshirt. Confronted by dials and buttons he didn't understand, he called out, "Honey? Which setting am I supposed to use on the washing machine?" "Well, it depends," his wife shouted in response. "What does the label say?" There was a pause as he checked. Then he yelled back, "Extra large." For the joke to work, there has to be a widely accepted stereotype that makes the idea of men doing housework incongruous. And indeed, there's evidence that the division of chores still falls along the lines of what's traditionally considered "men's work" versus "women's work." A 2008 Gallup poll, for example, showed that husbands were far more likely to be responsible for the car and the yard, while wives took care of the housecleaning, laundry, and kids.[4]

It's true that as wives have increasingly moved into the workplace in recent decades, many husbands have begun to pick up the slack at home, but questions of fairness remain. It matters deeply. Researchers have found that in dual-earner couples, both husbands and wives who feel they're doing more than their fair share of the housework are less happily married and more likely to divorce.[5] Spouses who believe they're getting the short end of the deal may experience depression, distress, anger, or rage.[6]

But what's fair? It's not as simple as writing down every possible household chore and assigning half the list to each spouse. Other factors have to be considered. Given work responsibilities outside the home, how much time does each spouse have available? What skills does each spouse have? Which chores does each particularly like or dislike? Which allow more choice and control over when they can be done?[7] As responsibilities go, changing light bulbs is not on the same level as changing diapers. It's possible to let the first one go for a couple of days. The second one . . . well, you get the point.

Furthermore, we have to deal with the fact that spouses may not begin with the same ideals of fairness. Expectations rooted in one's cultural and family experience lead to deeply personal judgments about who's shirking and being a bad spouse. If the bride and groom are oblivious to their expectations and differences in that regard, they're more likely to make automatic and absolute judgments about the other person's unfairness and to suffer resentment.

Of course, bringing this discussion into the premarital preparation process doesn't mean locking couples into a lifelong and nonnegotiable agreement. Before a couple actually comes together in marriage, it's nearly impossible for them to anticipate all the demands that will be made on their time and energy, or the resources they will have to meet them. And couples may need to revisit the issue repeatedly as careers change and children grow. Your goal for this conversation, therefore, is not to establish some kind of contract regarding roles and responsibilities, but rather to help them have a good first discussion of the issues.

In general, what you're looking for in each couple's answers to the CJ are differences in their *experiences* that may give rise to differences in *expectations*. Marc, for example, grew up in a family where Dad was the sole wage earner and only had to take care of the yard work and anything "mechanical" at home, while Mom did everything else, including child care. The kids had a few responsibilities, such as cleaning their rooms once a week, but mostly were expected to focus on their schoolwork.

Both of Cleo's parents, however, worked full time. They constantly negotiated and renegotiated who should do what, on the basis of their shifting schedules. The kids were expected to carry their share of the load, with the older kids caring for their younger siblings, and everyone having some reasonable role in housecleaning and meal preparation.

What happens when Marc and Cleo marry? As suggested earlier, none of this may make much difference when responsibilities are easily manageable and no one is being pushed too far out of his or her comfort zone. He or she may experiment with new roles and do so gladly. But the test comes when one or both feel the pressure of having too many demands and not enough time. When hard choices have to be made, the implicit "shoulds" often take over. *You should help out more around the house. You should quit your job and take care of the kids. That's the right thing to do. Why can't you see that?* If they think or feel such things, even if they don't say them out loud, it will skew the conversation and make it harder for them to listen to each other.

To use what should be a familiar distinction by now, your task as coach is to focus primarily on the process by which they discuss their differences, and only secondarily on the content of any agreement they might make. Help them listen to each other's stories, explore their expectations, and understand each other, to establish a foundation upon which future marriage-strengthening conversations can be built.

Let's begin with the second question (see page 114) on the CJ, because it's the one that's more likely to raise some eyebrows. Partners are asked to envision what household responsibilities each of them might actually have in the marriage. The question is designed to get explicitly at their expectations, and may well be a point of contention and negotiation.

But the context for their answer here is the multipart question that comes before, which asks partners to explore their own memories of how responsibilities were handled in their families of origin. The list of chores presented at the beginning serves both as a memory aid and to make the more general point that a lot of things need to be done to keep a household running!

The various parts of the question are meant to be simple and nonthreatening, while providing potentially useful background to their unspoken expectations and preferences. As you read their responses, ask yourself questions such as the following:

- How traditional were their families in terms of gender roles? Did their fathers do traditionally male tasks around the house, and their mothers traditionally female tasks? Such experiences can have an unrecognized influence on each spouse's intrinsic sense of what's right or wrong in the division of labor. And note that the felt need can be either to reproduce or to resist the parents' pattern, to run toward it or away from it. Indeed, asking how their parents felt about the division of labor may be particularly illuminating.

- How much responsibility did they carry growing up? Did everyone pitch in as able, or did the parents do all the work? When it comes to maintaining a household, there may be more of a learning curve for some spouses to achieve an active and core sense of responsibility, in which they no longer feel like they're doing someone a favor.

- If there were chores they particularly disliked, was it more because of the nature of the work itself (e.g., cleaning up after the dog), or because of the way the responsibility was communicated (e.g., it had to be done to the exacting standards of an overly strict parent)?

You can ask the couple if they ever saw their parents negotiate responsibilities, and if so, how those conversations went. This helps provide even more context for talking about the emotional reasons that partners have the expectations and preferences that they do. Without some such explicit conversation, unvoiced and unmet expectations are apt to become more insistent when the couple feels cornered by circumstances such as the increase of responsibility that comes with the birth of children or a change of jobs. Spouses become more insistent and less able to listen, leading to cycles of conflict that erode their trust in each other.

Working Outside the Home

Since the 1950s—the heyday of the male breadwinner/female homemaker ideal—the percentage of men in the American workforce has steadily decreased, while the reverse has been true for women. The proportion of women who work is projected to stay above half for the foreseeable future.[8] In a steadily increasing number of households, the wife is the primary wage earner, prompting couples to seriously reevaluate their expectations and commitments regarding gender roles, work, and family life.[9]

But what role models did the partners have growing up? Did one or both parents work? How was that work understood? Most American families now depend on two incomes; the reality of married life in a shifting cultural environment is that many couples are negotiating arrangements that may be quite different from what they're used to. It's important to have that perspective entering the conversation.

The third question (see page 114) asks about family history at two levels. Partners are asked to describe which family members worked and how much, but are also asked to reflect on the meaning attached to that work. In some cases, work outside the home represents a "career," implying work that is of personal significance and expected to be long term. It's not just about the money. In other cases, work *is* primarily about the money. Family members may have been forced by circumstances to contribute in whatever way they could to the household income, or may have taken on various jobs to earn some spending cash or "fun money."

As with the question about household responsibilities, the couple's memories of the past may exert both a pull and a push, both "This is the way it should be" and "It will never be that way again!" Remembering his perennially stressed-out mother, a husband may declare to himself, *No wife of mine will ever have to work*, and believe that he is failing as a provider if she does. It may be hard for him to imagine that his wife actually *wants* a career, a desire that will naturally have important implications for the division of labor.

Thus, instead of asking the controversial question of who will or won't work outside the home after they're married, we've taken a more positive route. Question 4 (see page 114) frames the conversation as one between two people who each have hopes and dreams and need each other's support, and question 3 gives some background context. Help the couple stay within that conversational frame, coaching each partner to cogently and congruently express his or her desires while the other compassionately listens.

Expect this conversation to overlap with the one about money. Ideas about who should or shouldn't work in the family, and how money is to be controlled and spent, are often closely tied with a sense of being personally valued (or devalued!) by one's partner. It would be prudent, as you prepare for your first meeting, to read these answers in tandem.

Making Time for Marriage

Finally, couples enjoying the romantic aura of courtship may find it hard to envision a day in which their relationship becomes routine. But that's exactly what happens for many. They get so busy with work, inside and outside the home, that the marriage relationship itself is taken for granted. Schedules seem determined by necessity: food needs to get on the table; children need to be tucked into bed; bills need to be paid. Who has time for anything else?

Marriage preparation provides a crucial opportunity to impress upon the couple the importance of *making time* for the relationship. You are coaching them in constructive communication to help them deal with differences. The same skills will also help them build closeness even when there are no differences to negotiate. There are gender stereotypes of wives who long to have meaningful conversation with their stoically silent husbands, but the reality for couples in which both spouses work full time is that their "busy lives don't give them as much time as they'd like for communication."[10] Help them make the time.

Recall the discussion in chapter 5 about the importance of positivity in the marriage, and the supporting exercise in appendix E, "Making Our Marriage Stronger." Question 5 (see page 114) has a similar purpose. Asking for warning signs may prompt memories of their parents' relationship, or observations about times in their present relationship when they feel taken for granted. As always, help them to listen well to each other's stories. If possible, use their individual ideas about behaviors to which they would be willing to commit to come up with a shared and proactive plan. Coach them to be realistic (they can't have date night every night!) and concrete enough that anyone would be able to understand exactly what they're committing to do. And remember: helping them plan one simple thing that they actually succeed at doing is better than having a more complex and comprehensive plan that dies of frustrated neglect.

Additional Resources

- **Book:** David and Claudia Arp and Curt and Natelle Brown, *10 Great Dates Before You Say "I Do"* (Grand Rapids: Zondervan, 2003).

  The *10 Great Dates* curriculum leads couples through ten marriage-building discussions on a variety of topics. Date number eight in this version of the curriculum helps couples decide how to share household chores. See also the related website www.marriagealive.com, which has similar resources for married couples and empty nesters.

•**Book:** Willard Harley, *His Needs, Her Needs: Building an Affair-Proof Marriage,* rev. ed. (Grand Rapids: Revell, 2011).

In chapter 10, Harley presents a process for creating a fair division of labor that provides a useful place to begin. Harley also makes the important point that the real test comes with how a couple handles the tasks that neither partner wants to do, making it an issue not only of fairness but also of love.

C h a p t e r
E i g h t

Love and Affection

Love and romance. What associations do those words bring to mind? Together, they define a large part of what we imagine to be good in life, particularly when it comes to marriage. But some couples assume that all of this will come naturally and that they don't need to talk about it. They simply follow the Nike mantra to "just do it," relying on conventional wisdom, popular culture, past experience, and relational trial and error.

A couple's intimate life together should be understood as an organic part of their relationship, a shared expression of togetherness. All couples must find effective ways to communicate about their physical and sexual needs and expectations, an ongoing and evolving conversation that can be challenging even for the most experienced couples. This became clear to me (Jim) when my wife Louise and I were leading a marriage retreat where we were asked to participate in separate panel discussions. Men were herded into one room set up like a sports bar, and women gathered in another room set for afternoon tea. The focus of discussion in both rooms was the same: sex.

The topic may have been predictable, but the outcome was surprising. During a luncheon, my wife, Louise, shared with the women a story of how we found that we had to be more intentional about finding time together in a houseful of young children. We affectionately used the code words *on night* and *off night* to signal to each other our intentions for a rendezvous later that day. Somehow the group misunderstood as an expectation what Louise intended as a tip. "Are you saying every other day? You've got to be kidding," said one woman, alarmed. Word spread quickly. Within the hour I was greeted by a group of men who cheered and offered me high fives. Apparently, they appreciated the message.

Talking about sexual issues can be tricky. Even the most intentional couples can find their physical relationship lacking in spontaneity, frequency, and vitality when they fail to communicate effectively about what they want and need. You might think that couples anticipating marriage would be in a different category, but in fact, their need for communication and understanding is just as great, if not more so.

Marital intimacy involves so much more than sex. It requires ongoing verbal and nonverbal messages that say, "You're special," "You're unique," and "I've chosen to be with you, and only you." Jack and Judy Balswick suggest that for Christians especially, love and sex require a relationship characterized by acts of love, acceptance, empowerment, and intimate knowing.[1] Couples who "just do it" often lack what they need to fulfill both the promise and purpose of the sexual relationship that God intended: not just procreation, but also pleasure and the fulfillment of physical and emotional needs.[2] In marriage, physical and sexual closeness can be a celebration of God's creative intent, and our hope is that you might help couples enjoy that kind of intimacy by making affection intrinsic to making love.

Communication is essential to building a deep bond of emotional and physical intimacy. Couples who find ways to confidently discuss expectations and needs can be more responsive to the changes that occur in their relationship over time. Without this, sex can become the defining issue in a marriage. Experts estimate that sex plays a 15 to 20 percent role in a couple's overall happiness when they are doing well, but 50 to 70 percent when they are in distress.[3] A couple must be able to talk openly and honestly about their experiences, bodies, and needs if physical affection and sex are to be a source of true intimacy and joy.

Talking about sex can be a challenge for some partners—as well as some pastors—and sexual expectations and concerns can take center stage for couples around their wedding day. Because misunderstanding and fear can sabotage the conversation, we've put together a set of questions to help couples talk about love and affection as an everyday part of their relationship.

Expressing Physical Affection

Expressions of affection are shaped by one's culture and generation, and by personal preferences. Some partners are more directly demonstrative (e.g., using words of endearment, hugging, touching), whereas others are more indirect (e.g., giving gifts, meeting physical needs). Couples may bring very different histories of expressing affection to their relationship. Getting them to talk about what they observed growing up gives them a way to identify possible differences in values and expectations, as well as their own "vocabulary" of affection.[4]

Intimacy is not the same thing as having identical wishes and expectations. Couples embody the image of God when they are able to express their uniqueness and at the same time grow toward unity, integrating their differences into a common bond.[5] Help partners normalize their differences and invite them to explore what it means to weave them together in love and faith, like a three-stranded cord that is not easily broken (Eccles. 4:12).

Question 1 (see page 115) asks couples to reflect (a little humorously at first) on the ways they have seen their own parents express physical affection. Such conversations can highlight fond memories and positive experiences of being loved, or trigger painful moments of loss and estrangement. An adult from a divorced home, for example, may focus more on what *wasn't* shared than what was.

When coaching, it can be helpful to focus differently on positive and negative experiences. When a partner shares about positive experiences of affection, you can prompt further discussion by asking him or her to say more about its impact on the family's life. For those who share more painful memories, empathy and support are important. You can then encourage the partner to share what he or she wishes would have been different. Talking about what the person needed back then can open the discussion to what he or she might hope for in his or her marriage.

If memories are significantly difficult for partners to discuss, consider suggesting further conversation with a therapist who can help them understand the impact of family history on one's expectations of marriage. Some families have been abusive, and physical touch has been a source of pain; partners with these past issues should seek additional support, particularly if they have not sought help in the past.

The second question (see page 115) highlights perceived differences in how the partners evaluate the affection they already share. Each partner's expectations shape not only his or her experience of the relationship but also of himself or herself. In moments of uncertainty, a partner can wonder if he or she is desirable, and will ultimately fear rejection. Reacting to this fear, the other partner may pull away, heightening the tension between them. This is a common pattern for distressed couples, one that can be particularly painful when their sexual relationship is on the line.

Consider the husband who believed that his wife's desire for him was a direct indication of his importance to her. He expected that she would want to have sex as often as he did, and when she felt differently, he took her response as a personal rebuff. Exploring his feelings of rejection, he was better able to separate his need for affirmation from his expectation that they have sex daily. She, in turn, was relieved to know that his frustration was about more than just hormones. His daily pursuit of her had become a turnoff, and knowing more about his desire for affirmation opened the door to a new conversation that brought them closer together.

Some couples will seem quite content with the physical affection in their relationship, for a variety of reasons. If it seems that their answers point to an area of strength, say so, and use it as an opportunity for them to express appreciation to each other.

Communicating Desires and Expectations

Couples may assume that because they love each other they should automatically know what the other needs and wants; they "mind read" what their partner thinks and expects, without any direct input. Or, they avoid conversations about physical intimacy and sexual pleasure because it feels too awkward to express their likes and dislikes openly.

Couples may have similar needs for intimacy but different preferences for how it's to be expressed.[6] For many women the path to sexual intimacy is through emotional connection, whereas for many men the path to emotional connection is through sexual intimacy.[7] Successful couples develop ways to communicate about their differences, value their shared uniqueness, and express closeness.

In question 3 (see pages 115–16), we ask couples to reflect on ways they express nonsexual affection, to lower the bar of difficulty for this conversation. Even so, expect it to feel awkward for them—especially for those who can't imagine talking about such things to a pastor! The point is that if a couple finds it difficult to talk to each other about their likes and dislikes at this level, they will find it even more challenging to express their preferences in their sexual relationship. The key is finding verbal and nonverbal ways of communicating what is pleasing to them.[8] This requires a sense of teamwork and a willingness for each partner to put the other partner's needs ahead of his or her own. Here is one way of sharing this idea: "Sometimes this means giving pleasure in a way that fits your partner's wishes, and at other times helping your partner know what is pleasing to you. Both are a way of giving."

Question 4 (see page 116) bridges from their expression of affection in general to their sexual relationship in particular. The discussion may have already moved in that direction; if not, you can fold the concerns they have here into the conversation below.

Preparing for the Reality

The hard reality is that difficulties in a sexual relationship are quite common. Couples may assume that they will be good at sex from the start or can "just do it" according to their natural desires. But it's been estimated that more than three-fourths of all couples will have to confront a sexual issue at some point in their marriage.[9] This includes disagreements over sexual preferences (e.g., positions; oral sex), frequency and quality, and other related issues (e.g., infertility; discomfort related to illness).

The couples you see for marriage preparation may vary tremendously in their history of sexual involvement, but they all need realistic psychological, physical, and relational expectations. Without recognizing it, couples may subscribe to common but misleading and unhelpful myths about what's normal or expected in terms of physical endowment, "drive," and orgasm.[10] Measuring themselves against such unrealistic standards, they saddle themselves and each other with a sense of frustration, disappointment, or failure in one of the most vulnerable areas of marriage.[11]

Aligning expectations with reality helps reduce disappointment and the pressure to perform. For example, researchers have found that "regular couples" (those having sex once or twice a week) reported that sex was "very good" 20 to 25 percent, "good" 40 to 60 percent, "fair" 15 to 20 percent, and "dissatisfying" 5 to 15 percent of the time.[12] The typical couple rarely strikes out, but they don't necessary hit a home run each time either. You don't have to challenge expectations directly if this is beyond your comfort zone, but you may want to point couples to other resources if you find them holding unrealistic expectations.

For other issues that involve unresolved hurts and fears regarding past sexual history, it's wise to have names of qualified mental health professionals ready to offer as a resource. Your openness and nonjudgmental concern will make it more likely that they will actually seek the help they need. Remember that sexual and relational problems are mutually reinforcing, so providing a place to identify problems early can make a difference over the life of their marriage, even if you are not the one helping them directly with these issues.

The Jumpstarter primes couples to reflect on and discuss three sensitive and potentially divisive areas of their intimate life together. The first, addressed in question 5 (see page 116), is their concerns about the wedding night. Making space for them to express such worries in advance gives them time to explore solutions and helps guard against misunderstanding and performance anxiety. The wedding night itself is not the time to try to solve difficulties! Indeed, suggesting to couples the general wisdom of not discussing problems during lovemaking can give them permission both to have problems and to discuss them at a more opportune time.

Both Maria and George were coming into the marriage with no prior sexual experience. He was eager for their wedding night, and privately felt miffed that she didn't seem to be as excited as he was. Discussing what she wrote on the Jumpstarter, Maria admitted that she felt shy about undressing in front of George. When he succeeded in listening empathically, George realized that he had been taking this personally, and now that he understood, he somehow liked this quality in her. They agreed that, for a while at least, she would undress privately and get into the bed, and then George would join her.

The second area of discussion is birth control. The two parts of question 6 (see page 116) will give you a quick read of whether they have a plan and how satisfied they are with the way the plan was decided. If a couple already has a shared plan in which they are confident, you can encourage them by asking how they reached their decision, affirming any use of good communication skills. If one or both partners are dissatisfied with the way the decision was made, ask them to discuss how things could have been done differently. This may lead, of course, to a new conversation about the plan itself, so be prepared to coach accordingly. It can be helpful to explore their assumptions about who has responsibility for the decision, as well as the level of information they have about various methods.

There is no absolutely foolproof method of contraception, save complete abstinence or surgery, so couples should be aware of the advantages and disadvantages of each. For example, hormonal contraceptives, such as the Pill, are more convenient for the man but can create unpleasant side effects for the woman, as well as leaving her feeling that contraception is her responsibility alone. This illustrates the balance of concerns involved. Overall, as a symbol of their unity, birth control should ideally be a shared decision. In addition, if a method is inconvenient or unpleasant to one or both partners, couples may be inconsistent in its use, particularly if they haven't explicitly discussed the issues.

We don't assume that you will be the one to provide the information they need. Point them to their family physician or OB/GYN, especially if medical concerns come up in the conversation, or direct them to the resources listed at the end of the chapter.

Discussions about birth control can also be opportunities to reflect on their hopes and dreams for their future. Don't be surprised, therefore, if talk veers toward issues related to parenting and children; be prepared to direct the conversation into their responses to section 4 (parenting) of the CJ as needed, beginning with questions 3 and 4. Procreation is literally a life-giving result of their sexual relationship. This can put the discussion on a different footing, inviting both partners to think about the future through the steps they are taking today.

Question 7 (see page 117) addresses the third area of discussion: sexual attraction to someone else. This question may catch some couples off guard, but we encourage them to consider how they will handle the everyday realities of sexual desire. In traditional wedding vows, the bride and groom pledge to forsake all others as long as they both shall live; they are making a covenant commitment to a lifelong, exclusive sexual relationship. But the sexual feelings we have as men and women are not by nature monogamous.

This discussion may unearth feelings of jealousy and allegations of flirtatious behavior. Recall the story of Marla and Jorge from chapter 2. Partners may have misunderstood each other's behavior, and unless they've had constructive conversations, they may be harboring feelings of resentment that will influence their relationship going forward. You will need to be very active to coach them both to speak and listen appropriately.

Help couples make the distinction between having a feeling and acting on it. Normalizing feelings of attraction can free the partners to find more constructive ways to handle them; mere denial or suppression can ironically reinforce the feelings. However, be careful to avoid normalizing one partner's feelings at the expense of another's. "All guys stare at attractive women," for example, may be an inappropriate, nonlistening response to a woman's feelings of jealousy. Unless you have reason to believe that one partner is excessively possessive of the other, reframe such feelings as expressing the desire for faithful exclusivity, and listen for the fears beneath them. A partner's words of reassurance help couples face the insecurity that such situations can trigger. Coach them through a conversation about what concrete steps they can take as individuals to responsibly honor each other's feelings and their covenant relationship.

Additional Resources

- **Book:** Jack Balswick and Judy Balswick, *Authentic Human Sexuality: An Integrated Approach*, 2nd ed. (Downers Grove, IL: InterVarsity Press, 2008).

A helpful discussion of key issues from a psychological and theological perspective, and a key resource for pastors wanting a broader discussion of sexuality and Christian life.

•**Book:** Clifford L. Penner and Joyce J. Penner, *Getting Your Sex Life Off to a Great Start: A Guide for Engaged and Newlywed Couples* (Nashville: Thomas Nelson, 1994).

An accessible, nonthreatening, and practical approach. Great for couples who are looking to prepare for their wedding night.

•**Book:** Clifford L. Penner and Joyce J. Penner, *The Gift of Sex* (Nashville: W Publishing Group, 2003).

Full of practical instruction and written from a thoroughly Christian perspective, this book provides a comprehensive reference for addressing common sexual issues and inspiring couples to celebrate sex as a gift from God.

C h a p t e r
N i n e

The Meaning of Money

It's a commonplace that the Bible has more to say about money and wealth than nearly any other topic. That's understandable, considering that the root issue is actually idolatry. Recall these familiar words from the Sermon on the Mount: "Do not store up for yourselves treasures on earth. . . . But store up for yourselves treasures in heaven. . . . For where your treasure is, there your heart will be also" (Matt. 6:19-21). A more literal translation of Jesus' words would be "Don't treasure up treasures." That way of reading it, though redundant, suggests that Jesus cared more about the verb than noun—the act of treasuring rather than the treasure itself.

And in the very next passage (Matt. 6:25-34), Jesus deals with the matter of anxiety, teaching that it is faithless to worry about such basic needs as food and clothing. Instead, we are to trust in God's loving concern and "seek first his kingdom and his righteousness" (v. 33), knowing that God will take care of the rest. In what do we place our security? That will always be the backdrop to pastoral conversations about money.

All couples, Christian or not, relate to money on the basis of a complex array of spiritual, social, and psychological factors. Take gender: there's some evidence that men and women approach money differently. Men seem more likely to take financial risks, and this may be because they're also more likely to see money as an arena of competition.[1] That's *not* to say that all men are one way and women are another. But it does suggest that we shouldn't be surprised when two engaged people approach money matters differently.

It's not just about balancing income and expenses. Money can have a different *meaning* for one partner than it does for the other, symbolizing security, independence, trust, or self-worth. That's why, as researchers in the field of "neuroeconomics" have argued, when it comes to money, we're just not as rational as we would like to believe.[2]

Not surprisingly, when researchers ask couples what they argue about, the number one problem is often money. As David Olson and his colleagues have written:

If you sometimes feel as though financial issues dominate your life, you are not alone. It is estimated that we spend up to 80 percent of our waking hours earning money, spending money, or thinking about money. A survey conducted by American Express Financial Advisors revealed that 66 percent of Americans spend more time thinking about money and careers than they do about sex, health, or relationship. What's more, financial issues are the most common source of stress for couples and families. . . . Money problems are now second only to infidelity as a cause of divorce.[3]

Happy and unhappy couples alike argue about money. Moreover, one research team found that compared to other topics, money-related arguments were longer, more fraught with negative emotions, and less likely to be either handled well or resolved.[4] That's because, as another team of authors has put it: "Money, like nothing else we know of, is the screen on which couples project all their deepest fears, hopes, dreams, and hurts in life."[5] No wonder it's at the root of so many arguments.

We could do engaged couples a great service by helping them prepare for some of the challenges. Here are the issues addressed by the Conversation Jumpstarter.

Spending Versus Saving

One bride-to-be grew up in a family that budgeted carefully for anticipated expenses. Only when a specified amount had been laid aside, plus a little extra "for a rainy day," could the remainder be spent on nonbudgeted items—and even then within limits. For the groom, however, money was to be *enjoyed.* That doesn't mean a Luke 15 kind of prodigality, but rather a spirit of generosity and play; he loved to spend money on fun gifts for others. He understood the importance of saving, but for him, enjoyment was a higher value than security. For her, it was the other way around. And when it looked like their budget would be tight, his need for enjoyment and her need for security both went up.

People approach money—and scarcity—differently. When money seems in short supply, one spouse may have an almost primal urge to hoard, while the other feels, *Spend it now while you have a chance.* But that's just an exaggerated version of the meanings and emotions that are there even when things are going well: *This is what I need in order to feel secure about tomorrow* versus *This is what I need in order to feel like it's worth getting out of bed today.*

Again, how couples save or spend, or react to each other's financial habits, reveals something of their underlying assumptions about the meaning of money. What do I need, in terms of money or what it can buy, to be happy? To feel successful? To feel like I have enough control over my life? To have the acceptance and recognition of others? To feel cared for? To be able to show my generous nature? Pragmatic disagreements about whether this or that is a better value for the price are one thing. Chronic disagreements about money habits, however, usually point to some unmet underlying need. Engaged couples can benefit from beginning to recognize such "hidden issues" in themselves and each other.[6]

Question 1 (see page 118) on the money section of the Jumpstarter will help you get a sense of the couple's spending and saving habits. The upper choices reflect a preference for spending over saving; the lower choices reflect the opposite. Of course, people are not simply "spenders" or "savers" all the time, but may have persistent tendencies that either match or contradict those of their spouse-to-be.

If differences come up during the session, ask them to reflect on their preferences out loud, and to listen to each other's. Help them explore the hidden issues that lie beneath their habits and tendencies. A place to start would be to encourage them to tell stories about their response to question 6 (see page 119). Use curiosity to make connections and open the door for further reflection: "Gail, your story about how your father gambled away the family's money is really powerful. I am wondering how that might be connected to the way you budget every dollar so carefully, or how you feel about the way Mike uses his credit cards." Remember, the primary goal here is self- and mutual understanding, not problem solving.

Be listening for what seem like unreasonable extremes, such as careless and compulsive spending or Scrooge-like hoarding. These are not things you can fix, but you can draw their attention to the dangers (e.g., out-of-control accumulation of debt; resentment and anxiety; a failure to deal with legitimate needs). As always, frame your comments in terms of your concern for their relationship, and stand ready with an appropriate referral as needed.

Differences in spending and saving habits can easily cause ongoing friction in a marriage. But differences aren't the only issue. As one consultant has written: "The most financially fatal combination is two spenders."[7] When their spending habits go unchecked, these couples rack up debt more quickly, continually pay high interest rates on revolving credit, have little to no cushion for emergencies, and do a poor job of saving for their retirement years. And while one might worry less about the combination of two savers, they too can fall into their own "trap of being too cheap, forgoing fun for frugality."[8] It's good to be disciplined about the present, and cautious about the future. But especially in those early years of marriage, the couple should also be enjoying their time together. You don't have to convince them to stop being frugal; just encourage them to budget in some fun.

Debt

One practical but thorny issue that engaged couples should discuss involves debt. Does either of them owe money? How much? To whom? Couples need to be financially transparent with each other before they commit to forming a single household with a common budget.

Some form of indebtedness is the norm. Take credit cards as an example. One 2012 report estimates that nearly half of all American households carry some balance on their credit cards from month to month, and that the average amount owed is more than $15,000.[9] So how much debt are engaged couples bringing into their union? And what difference does it make?

In one study, researchers discovered that 70 percent of the more than one thousand couples surveyed brought debt into the marriage; half of these owed $5,000 or more (not including home mortgages). Automobile loans were the most common kind of debt, followed by credit card balances, school loans, and medical bills. Most important, compared to those who owed nothing, those who brought even as little as $1,000 of debt into married life scored significantly lower on measures of marital adjustment and satisfaction.[10] The more a couple's debt increases, the less time they spend together and the more they argue about money. Conversely, those who pay off their debts also seem to reap the reward of improved marital satisfaction.[11] So shouldn't couples think twice before going into hock to finance a lavish wedding?

Questions 3 to 5 (see pages 118–19) ask couples to be honest about the amount of debt they're bringing into the marriage. If they've done their homework, you'll have their total debt, monthly debt payments, and monthly income to compare. There is such a thing as an unreasonable amount of debt, and couples shouldn't naively saddle themselves with that kind of burden when they're trying to build a new and stable relationship.

Banks use a debt-to-income (DTI) ratio to determine who's a good candidate for a loan, and this is one way to estimate how much debt is too much.[12] But you don't need to play the role of financial expert. Start with a commonsense comparison of the numbers on each of their answer sheets and then compare their answer sheets to each other. Are you concerned? Do they seem to be worried about their own finances or each other's? If not, should they be?

If you're concerned, say so, and frame it as a matter of their relationship: "I've noticed that the amount you're spending each month to service your debts seems really high compared to the money you're bringing in. At least it seems high to me! I'm worried about the kind of strain that might put on your marriage, especially when you're just starting out, in the foundational years of your relationship. I'm wondering if you're worried about that, too."

Probe gently, if necessary. Who's continuing to take on more debt? Who's maxed out his or her credit cards, scraping by on the minimum payment? Who's counting on some vague or uncertain new source of income? You don't have to give the couple solutions. Calmly state your own concerns, help them discuss their concerns, and point them to resources that may help, such as the ones listed at the end of this chapter.

But again, it's not just about numbers. Strong feelings may come out here because of the personal meanings behind the numbers. Remember Bill and Sue from chapter 5? Having grown up with a financially irresponsible father, Bill has a gut-level need for financial security. What Sue might consider a reasonable level of indebtedness may feel reckless to him. Unless they recognize this, their arguments about practical matters of dollars and cents will go around and around in endless, frustrating circles.

In such a case, your job would be to help them have a relationship-building conversation about his fear. Help her listen to his story nondefensively until he feels understood. Then encourage him to listen to her story so that he understands how their experiences, and therefore their values, are different.

Financial Partnership

Let's be honest. Money can bring out the worst in people, even dividing families (e.g., see Luke 12:13-21). That's why attorneys advocate wills and living trusts. It's not only to avoid probate, but also to protect families from themselves. They also encourage engaged couples to consider prenuptial agreements that would protect individual assets in the case of divorce. This isn't just a matter of thinking, *You only married me for my money*; people getting remarried, for example, may want to ensure their inheritance goes to children from a prior marriage. But most couples don't do it, partly because they don't really believe that they *will* divorce, and partly because they don't want to send negative signals at the beginning of their relationship.[13]

This points us to another meaning dimension: how we handle money says something about our commitment to each other and to the marriage. For example, what does it mean if a husband spends $500 out of a joint account without consulting his wife? What does it mean if she insists on keeping a bank account that only has her name on it?

The issues are complex, and there's no universal benchmark, biblical or otherwise, for determining the boundaries between "his" money, "her" money, and "their" money. But we like the way Patty Howell and Ralph Jones have put it:

> To the extent that you can, set up your organizational system for handling money with your partner so that you have a sense of being "in it" together. It's okay to have some separate funds. However, don't overlook the opportunities for emotional closeness that can result from having money as a mutual cornerstone of your partnership. ("We've saved enough for a down payment!" "We've got enough for a vacation!") Sharing money and sharing decisions about its use give you the opportunity to nurture your feelings of being close, of being together.[14]

We would go further. "Being in it together" is more than just a feeling of closeness. It's a tangible expression of commitment to each other and to marriage as a covenant partnership. That doesn't mean that all money must be held in joint accounts; it may make better budgetary sense to have some "his" and "her" discretionary funds. But even *that* decision should be made jointly, and there should be *some* money that is "theirs" together, for the sake of shared goals.

Help couples discuss their responses to question 2 (see page 118) as needed. From the standpoint of financial responsibility, there are no intrinsically right or wrong answers. Someone who insists on unsupervised spending may be looking for license to do what he or she pleases, but it's also possible that he or she really is trustworthy and has been insultingly micromanaged in the past.

From a relationship standpoint, however, such an attitude may signal an unwillingness to be open to the other person's concerns; that bodes poorly for the couple's sense of partnership. Help them come to tentative agreements about joint versus individual accounts (use appendix F, if necessary), and expectations about mutual accountability, for example, how much one spouse can spend without checking with the other first. Watch their reactions: issues of trust, independence, and control may surface here. Be diligent in helping them apply their constructive communication skills. Remind them that such agreements can be renegotiated but that ongoing commitment to some shared agreement is a way of reducing misunderstanding and increasing trust.

Use their answers to question 7 (see page 119) to also build their sense of partnership. Help each partner to dream aloud, and as you do, look for places where the other partner seems to share the dream in some way: "Frank, I noticed that you smiled and nodded when Annette started talking about going back to school for her MBA. I'm wondering what you were thinking about just then." Maybe he's been dreaming of going back to graduate school himself. Or maybe he thinks that an MBA would be the perfect thing for her career. Either way, it's something to build on as you help them take turns speaking and listening.

In rare cases, neither individual wants to hold any money jointly. Listen carefully to understand their resistance and then gently share the symbolic importance of some kind of financial partnership for their relationship: "I think I can see why it's important to both of you to keep your money separate. At the same time, I believe God intended marriage to be an intimate and trusting relationship. Can we see if we can figure out some goal or dream that you can share together as a symbol of your union?" Try using question 7 to spur them to think creatively of at least one goal that they could "invest in" together, and help them outline a plan.

Additional Resources

- **Website:** Crown Financial Ministries, http://crown.org

  Crown is the result of a merger in 2000 between the ministries of Christian financial experts Larry Burkett and Howard Dayton. Not everyone agrees with the organization's view that the Bible teaches that Christians should be debt free. Their website, however, offers a wealth of practical resources, including short publications available in print and e-book formats; free online articles on budgeting, debt, and other financial issues; and church/ministry resources, including free articles on pastors' finances.

- **Website:** Certified Financial Planner Board of Standards, Inc., http://www.cfp.net

  The CFP Board is the regulatory agency governing the certification of financial planners. Links on their website allow visitors to locate a local CFP or verify an individual's certification. If you don't already have a trusted CFP in your area to whom you would refer members of your congregation, this is a way to begin looking for one.

- **Book:** Natalie H. Jenkins et al., *You Paid How Much for That? How to Win at Money without Losing at Love* (San Francisco: Jossey-Bass, 2002).

This is one of our favorite books for couples on money matters from the people behind the well-known PREP marital enrichment program (https://www.prepinc.com); it helps couples identify hidden expectations and meanings, talk them out, and learn practical money management skills.

Chapter
Ten

The Possibilities of Parenthood

As mentioned earlier, my wife and I (Cameron) hail from different cultures. We also come from different-sized families; I am the youngest of two, while she is the eldest of five. We always knew we wanted children, but differed on the number. Not surprisingly, she envisioned us with five kids, while two seemed about right to me. As it turned out, circumstances made the decision: after two very difficult pregnancies, we were done.

Couples approaching parenthood have preconceived (no pun intended) ideas about what it will be like to be parents. How many children will they have, if any? How will they be disciplined, and who will do it? How much will each parent be involved in the day-to-day raising of the kids? What's the best way to teach values? To toilet train? The questions are endless, and spouses frequently have different perspectives—some realistic, some not. As the seventeenth-century English poet and satirist John Wilmot once said, "Before I got married, I had six theories about bringing up children; now I have six children, and no theories."[1]

Why consider such things at the front end of marriage? Because it's a well-established empirical fact: for many couples, the transition into parenthood is difficult. A recent review of nearly one hundred studies confirmed small but significant differences between couples with and without children: parents, especially those with babies or more than one child, were less satisfied in their marriages.[2] Granted, this should all be taken with a grain of salt, since there are studies suggesting that marital satisfaction declines over time whether children are present or not.[3] Moreover, there is evidence that the decline levels out after a while, and even reverses when the kids go off to school.[4]

Nevertheless, raising kids tests the resources of the marriage. On the one hand, a strong relationship can be made stronger if husband and wife meet the challenges together. On the other hand, becoming parents can exacerbate conflicts that already exist.[5] To those who naively assume that having children will solve their marital problems or shore up a shaky relationship, researchers forewarn, "On average, this tactic will backfire, and all parties will suffer."[6]

The issues raised by becoming parents go hand in glove with those raised elsewhere in this book. Household roles (chapter 7) change as spouses redistribute responsibilities around caring for a new baby; the nature of intimacy (chapter 8) changes as couples become parents; extended family relationships (chapter 11) change as the spouses' parents now become grandparents. And though the couple may previously have been satisfied to leave differences in their spiritual commitments (chapter 12) to the realm of individual choice, this too may change as they begin to contemplate in what tradition they wish to raise their children.

And there's one more layer of complexity: if one or both of the spouses-to-be has been married before, he or she may be bringing children into the new relationship. This can be a minefield of unexpressed and conflicting expectations. As one bewildered stepfather has put it: "I have no idea how I'm supposed to behave. . . . Can I kiss my wife in front of my stepchildren? Do I tell my stepson to do his homework, or is that exceeding my authority? Can I have my own kids over for the weekend . . . ? It's hard living in a family where there are no clear rules or lines of authority."[7]

For these reasons, one section of the Conversation Jumpstarter is devoted to expectations related to having and caring for children. The issues raised are deep. Some will think lovingly of one or both of their parents as role models. Others will say, "I never want to treat my own children the way my parents treated me." And they will bring these experiences and emotions with them into their conversation with each other and with you.

Again, your task is to create a safe environment for them to explore these issues with each other. There may be opportunities for you to do a little gentle teaching, but your primary goal is to help them forge a closer relationship by listening attentively to each other's stories and expectations. Here are some of the talking points.

General History and Expectations

The first two questions (see page 120) in this section ask for general information, which in many cases will already be known to both partners. Question 1 is a simple way for you to get a sense of the size and complexity of the families they grew up in, while question 2 helps ensure that each spouse is fully aware of preexisting relationships; if one partner is a noncustodial parent, it's quite possible that the other partner hasn't met or doesn't know of one or more of the children from previous relationships. Taken together, these two questions are designed to provide some basic information that can serve as a springboard or reference point, while eliminating some large (and potentially unpleasant!) surprises down the road.

Questions 3 and 4 (see page 120) put three simple expectations out on the table: whether each partner *wants* kids, and if so, when and how many. If they're tentative about their answers, reassure them that the purpose is merely to "take their temperature" on the matter, to see if there are differences in hopes and intentions that need to be discussed.

The answers to question 4 are likely to be negotiable; as the story at the beginning of the chapter suggests, the number itself may change dramatically when it's no longer in the realm of theory! Here, the main point is to get a quick read of "small" versus "large" family expectations and to see how each partner reacts to what the other has written. Answers to other questions may help you direct the conversation: "Harold, I see that you grew up as an only child, but Maude, you grew up surrounded by a lot of brothers and sisters. What does your answer to question 4 say about the kind of family you hope to have?"

Depending on how well their answers agree, question 3 may generate more controversy. Be curious about their answers. It can be useful to know what's behind their not wanting to think about it yet, or their desire to adopt. And indeed, we know couples in which the wife wants children as soon as possible and the husband doesn't want children at all. In such cases, your task is not to guide them to a firm decision, but to help them listen past their distress to get at the feelings and experiences beneath the answers. They don't have to agree; they just have to try to understand. They may be uncomfortable with the tension, but don't push for a premature resolution. Again, your focus as their coach is more on process than content. You can remind them instead of how important the issue is, encourage them to continue talking about it, and refer them to additional resources as needed.

Family-of-Origin Issues

For some individuals, having children is a natural extension of the love they experienced growing up. But others, as they become parents, try to right past wrongs. This is a deeper level of meaning associated with the possibility of parenthood. As Ellen Galinsky has written: "First-time parents-to-be remember the child they once were, and then form images centered around the way they would have liked their parents to treat them. . . . [They] have formed images of themselves as parents by recalling their own childhoods . . . [identifying] with the parent they will be and the child they were."[8]

Although many aspects of the couples' family-of-origin experience could be addressed, we've chosen to focus on two: how they were disciplined, and how close they felt to their parents. This reflects two major concepts in the popular and scientific literature on parenting: *control* (how parents direct a child's beliefs and behavior) and *warmth* or *support*. These are the cornerstones of psychologist Diana Baumrind's model of parenting, which was developed in the 1960s and is still influential today.[9]

In brief, Baumrind distinguished between three parenting styles: *authoritative* (high in control and support), *authoritarian* (high control but low support), and *permissive* (high support but low control). The permissive parent is consistently affirming but makes few if any demands that the child obey rules and standards. The authoritarian parent, by contrast, has a heavily top-down style that follows absolute standards to which the child is expected to adhere. At the extremes, both of these styles are problematic for the emotional well-being and social competence of the child.

The authoritative parent, however, is one who is warm and supportive, *and* has firm and consistent expectations of the child. Whereas the authoritarian parent tends to shut down discussion, authoritative parents tend to talk to and reason with their children. This points to a "commonsense" understanding of parenting as a two-way relationship in which the child's individuality is respected without the parents abdicating their authority.[10]

The research seems clear: some kind of authoritative parenting yields the best long-term outcomes.[11] Moreover, there is evidence that these are not just Western or "American" concepts but that they apply to other cultures as well.[12] In short, children seem to function best when their parents are warmly supportive and have clear expectations while avoiding intrusive forms of control.

Questions 5, 6, and 8 (see pages 120–21) raise the question of previous experiences and future expectations of discipline. Note, however, that we avoid using the word *discipline* until the last question, because some equate it with "harsh treatment." Those who had authoritative parents may even think they've never been "disciplined." We reserve the word, therefore, until question 8, where the more open-ended format allows for more information.

Question 5 is only for those who already have children. Have they already played the family role of disciplinarian? If so, how? If not, why not? Listen for themes of support and control, and for authoritative, authoritarian, and permissive patterns; compare their responses on question 5 to the stories they tell on question 8. (Note also that other responses to question 5 may be possible, as in a single-parent home where grandparents are the primary disciplinarians).

The point is that prior experiences will to some extent shape their expectations going forward: a sense of what works and what doesn't, of what to keep doing and what to change. Naturally, experiences of being parents in previous relationships will shape their expectations of parenthood in the new marriage. Comparing questions 5 and 6 will give you a sense of where they want continuity versus change, leaving you or the other partner to ask why as appropriate.

Pushing further back, how the partners' own parents treated them (question 8) will shape how they in turn treat their children. On the one hand, they may want to replicate their parents' example, or at least some parts of it. On the other hand, they may want to reject the old ways instead, correcting or compensating for what they perceive as their parents' mistakes. More subtly, they may consciously wish to discard some of their parents' methods (e.g., "I will never, never spank my child!"), but then find themselves doing the same or something similar (e.g., substituting verbal abuse for physical).

For the couple as individuals, whether they have children or not, use the responses to questions 5 through 8 together to get a preliminary sense of how earlier experiences relate to their image of what it will mean to be a parent now. Again, this is not for the purpose of diagnosis but of empathy. You are modeling openness, curiosity, and attentiveness, which become even more important when the spouses-to-be are having difficulty understanding each other's perspectives.

Stepfamily Issues

It's challenging enough for a couple to grow into their roles as parents when they start from scratch. It can be even more challenging in the case of remarriage. Images of the wicked stepparent abound in fairy tales and the popular imagination. Moreover, depending on the circumstances that led to the breakup of their family, children may not be ready to welcome a new mom or dad.

Indeed, children may not be wanting the parent-stepparent relationship to succeed at all: "In stepfamilies, children often feel a great sense of loss when their parent's new marriage is strengthened. It threatens their sense of family and the often-held fantasy of a parental reconciliation."[13] Weddings are supposed to be happy occasions, but the reality is that in remarriages, spouses and children alike are often dealing with grief and loss. Children may be angry, sullen, or resistant; stepparents may feel confused, hurt, or unappreciated. Small wonder, then, that new stepparents can be so confused about how to move forward: "If a stepfamily is to be successful, family members must reach a mutually satisfactory agreement on family roles and relationships, but there may be little initial consensus between parents, stepparents, and children on this issue."[14] It takes time for the family to build their new reality together. Much patience and good communication will be needed as all parties learn and adapt to differences in needs and expectations. The premarital preparation process is a good place to help establish some realistic expectations.

Following the recommendations in the earlier section, you will already have a sense of how family-of-origin issues may connect to past parental behaviors and future expectations. Again, your goal is to engage the couple in a conversation that promotes empathy and understanding. You're not expected to fix problems or to be an expert on stepfamily issues. But there are some simple things you can do for the couple to help shape healthier expectations of the road ahead.

First, try to normalize the difficulties.[15] Forming a stepfamily can be particularly complex, for example, if one or more of the children is entering adolescence. The teenager is needing or wanting more independence. However, at the same time, the adults may feel the need to draw the family closer together, to build a sense of unity. Both needs are legitimate, but they pull in opposite directions, leading to epic clashes and deeper hurt on both sides. The couple's practice of constructive communication will help, but these efforts have to be built on a solid base of realism—their family is not going to be the Brady Bunch. Ever. Encourage them to be patient with themselves and to have flexible and realistic expectations.

Second, teach stepparents to go slowly with their stepchildren, especially in matters of discipline. Authoritative parenting is a good thing with one's own biological children in a first marriage. And it can be good with stepchildren, but not right away.

Children are unlikely to accept the stepparent's authority at first; expect the transition to take a year or so.[16]

Thus, although we generally say that there are no "right answers" in the CJ, here we'll make an exception. Though it's not listed as one of the choices, the right answer to question 6 in the parenting section is, "It depends." In a blended family, especially at first, the primary responsibility for discipline lies with the biological parent. New spouses should focus on building warm, caring, patient relationships with their stepchildren, while supporting and deferring to the biological parent in matters of misbehavior.

That doesn't mean that the spouses can't disagree on parenting. But those differences should be negotiated in private. And as always, they should do so using good communication skills and relational thinking. Their shared goal is not to push their own preferences regarding parenting, but to work together for the health and stability of their new family, a worthy project that will require time and compromise.

Additional Resources

• **Website:** Smart Stepfamilies, http://www.smartstepfamilies.com

Founded by marriage and family therapist Ron Deal, this website provides links to numerous resources on stepparenting and stepfamily ministry, including books, free online articles, and schedules of conferences, webinars, and therapy intensives.

• **Website:** InStep Ministries, http://www.instepministries.com

A nonprofit ministry that aims to connect single and remarried parents with local church ministries. Resources include books and workbooks, free online articles, training and phone consultation for pastors, support groups, and marriage/remarriage preparation.

• **Online article:** Jean McBride, "Finding a Stepfamily Therapist," available at http://www.stepfamilies.info/quick-steps/QS_Finding_A_Therapist_D.pdf

A straightforward one-page handout for stepfamilies looking for a therapist.

• **Book:** Pamela L. Jordan, Scott M. Stanley, and Howard J. Markman, *Becoming Parents: How to Strengthen Your Marriage as Your Family Grows* (San Francisco: Jossey-Bass, 1999).

Another book from the people at PREP (www.prepinc.com), applying communication- and conflict-resolution skills to the transition into parenthood. Chapters help couples deal with underlying beliefs and expectations, preserve marital intimacy and friendship, handle fatigue and stress, and balance household responsibilities.

In-Laws and Extended Family

A wedding joins two people in marriage. The marriage, in turn, joins two families. Today, in America at least, most people choose whom they will marry, and their families do their best to support the decision. But this is not as easy as it may sound. Couples and their respective in-laws sometimes struggle to find ways to be a family with people to whom, all else being equal, they would not have chosen to be joined.

Over the years, social scientists have concluded that couples' adjustment to marriage is enhanced when they are able to be more autonomous from their families of origin.[1] Support for this view continues, even though little research is done on the role of in-laws in marriage. Not surprisingly, research has shown that newlyweds with lower levels of in-law conflict tend to be more satisfied in their relationships.[2] This appears to be true, however, not just in the initial adjustment period, but even two decades into marriage.[3] Most of the difficulties seem to be in mother/daughter and father/son in-law relationships, and these struggles can be more pronounced during life transitions such as the birth of a child.[4]

Stacey and Sean related differently to their families. He kept a comfortable distance from his parents, while she had a particularly close relationship with her mother, calling or texting her daily. Stacey's mother was strongly invested in her daughter's happiness and therefore in her marriage, which annoyed Sean at times. When Stacey told her mother about a fight between her and Sean, and Mom called to give Sean advice, he was incensed and accused Stacey of betraying their privacy. He felt their marriage issues were off limits to their parents and was offended that Stacey would be so open about their struggles. Stacey, confused by Sean's reaction, defended herself. Fortunately, the argument led the couple to make a more explicit agreement about privacy. Stacey promised to keep the best interests of their marriage in mind when talking with her mother, and the couple found better ways to manage their boundaries.

Genesis 2:24 is a favorite text for weddings: in marriage, a husband and wife leave their families, cleave to each other, and become one flesh. Analogously, couples move from depending on their families to depending on each other. "Leaving" is necessary to establishing a new identity as a couple, a relationship of giving and receiving in mutual dependence.[5]

At the same time, couples must find new ways to honor the role of parents in their lives, including showing kindness and caring for them in time of need.[6] Strong differences in cultural values may arise here, leaving partners mystified by each other's preferences. If, for example, the husband comes from a non-Western culture, his mother may expect to advise her new daughter-in-law on how to cook or to raise children. The wife may actively resent this, complaining to her husband and leaving him feeling divided in his loyalties.

An additional complication arises when spouses have family histories of neglect and abuse. Some individuals marry to escape a painful past, or hope that their new spouse will somehow shield them from further pain. Others hope their partners will meet emotional needs that weren't met in childhood; past violations of love and trust can carry over into a couple's relationship in ways that may be difficult to foresee.[7] Referring partners to professional therapy may be indicated when additional help is needed in effectively setting physical and emotional boundaries between the marriage and their families of origin.

The Jumpstarter helps couples reflect on issues that may arise with future in-laws. The questions explore themes of parental support, expectations, and blessings, identifying areas of both challenge and strength. Your role is to encourage partners to talk together about their experiences and expectations. Listen for differences, fears, and concerns. You can also take a positive approach by asking them what has worked thus far. It's important that both partners take responsibility for their own relationship with their parents.

Parental Support

Couples benefit when family members and friends lend practical and emotional support to the marriage. The first two CJ questions (see page 122) ask couples to reflect on how supportive they believe their respective parents are regarding their union.

Which parents support the marriage and which do not? Tom and Sheri may both rate his parents as "very supportive" and hers as "indifferent." But their perceptions might also disagree; Sheri might rate her parents as more supportive than Tom does, prompting questions as to why he would think this. Help the couple to be curious about these differences, and invite them to share a story or experience that illustrates their impressions. Some partners will find it difficult not to jump in mid-story and correct their partner's interpretations, so coach them to listen attentively.

Simply asking if they have discussed these differences before, and how they plan to address them, can open the conversation further. Normalizing the fact that such tensions are common, particularly when parents have been overinvolved in their children's lives, can help make room to discuss differences without having to deny or be threatened by them.

Boundaries

Success in marriage depends in part on how well partners are able to establish a new and clear sense of identity as a married couple. Jack and Judy Balswick describe this shared identity as a differentiated unity that is marked by a sense of God's purpose and an expression of self-giving growth.[8] Partners make sacrifices for the good of the marriage, at times putting their identity as an "us" ahead of their concerns as individuals.[9] This self-giving attitude helps couples navigate new in-law relationships.

This requires some psychological independence from their families, both as individuals and as a couple. Effective boundaries help couples maintain a balanced relationship of giving and receiving with their families of origin. Ineffective boundaries occur when a couple fails to set appropriate limits. But again, couples may have quite different values, and may disagree as to what "appropriate" means.

Sooner or later, a couple's decisions will affect members of the extended family, as in, "What do you mean you're not spending Christmas with us?" Such situations test how well a couple will balance their own interests with those of other family members in areas such as holiday planning, managing finances, and child rearing.

Questions 3 and 4 (see page 122) prompt partners for their expectations of giving and receiving emotional and financial support from their own parents, which may be rooted in cultural values, dynamics specific to each family, or both. Putting both partners' answers together will highlight the differences between them.

Couples must work through the two-sided theme of independence and dependence in their relationships with extended family. She might gratefully receive offers of financial help from her own parents as a sign of their love and concern, knowing that there are no strings attached. He, however, would rather die than ask his parents for money. Because such differences between partners may be rooted in deeply held values and assumptions, avoid making authoritative pronouncements as to what boundaries are appropriate. Instead, keep the decisions between them.

For example, you can ask partners for stories of sacrifices they have each made for their parents, and then ask them to reflect on what it would be like to make the same decision as a couple. Listen for hidden expectations as you simultaneously coach them to listen to each other. Extend the conversation by asking them to discuss appropriate limits: how much is too much to ask, or too much to give? If there is a related concrete decision the couple already needs to make in this area, consider using the method described in chapter 5.

Honoring Parents while Handling Expectations

Most of the focus of wedding preparation is on the couple, but usually, as suggested earlier, weddings also bring together two families. Couples need to be reminded that their story is part of a larger story—hopefully one mostly of love, caring, and faithfulness. All families have their limitations. Some families have endured significant challenges, while others have failed.

Regardless, parents never stop being parents; they have hopes and dreams for their children even as their children become adults. These hopes can translate into expectations about everything from kids to careers. These expectations, even when communicated with the best of intentions, can backfire, with the impact on the couple becoming the opposite of what was intended. Often the most difficult interactions, for example, happen between mothers-in-law and daughters-in-law when couples have their first child.

Setting boundaries and defining one's identity as a couple is best done in the context of a positive relationship with one's family, not in opposition to it. Each partner should have some responsibility for relating to and honoring his or her own parents (Exod. 20:12), instead of making the other spouse the go-between, a pattern that can escalate family and marital tensions. As Christians, both partners should make an active commitment to honoring both sets of parents, not only as a shared expression of their spiritual life, but also as a way of promoting positive emotions in the midst of changing expectations.

Questions 5 and 6 (see page 123) ask each partner to take an active and intentional role in supporting his or her spouse's relationship with his or her own parents. This requires each partner to step back and consider ways to promote a more positive relationship with each parent. These questions may be difficult for partners whose relationship with parents is strained. Here are a few suggestions for handling challenges you might encounter as coach.

First, some responses to the question will be too vague to put into practice. For example, Lance might say to Janie, "My father doesn't like to talk much. So don't take it personally; there's nothing much you can do." In this case, you can ask Lance for more concrete suggestions of what Janie *could* do: "So Lance, if your dad isn't talkative, what's one thing you would encourage Janie to do if she were sitting alone with him in a room?" In other words, focus on specific actions that can be taken in specific situations. If Lance needs more prompting, you can ask him what he has learned to do differently with his father that has improved their relationship. Even one small thing can be of help.

A second possible challenge arises when a partner gives advice in a way that seems to side with the parent and against the other partner. Janie might say to Lance, "My mother expects you to be prompt. If we are over for dinner, we need to be on time. That's something we'll have to work on." In this answer, Janie is implying not only that Lance is not punctual, but also that he needs to change to please her mother. Most likely, punctuality is not only important to Janie's mother, but also to Janie—in which case the real issue may be between the couple, rather than between Lance and his future mother-in-law.

Look for nonverbal cues that suggest a negative response from Lance, such as crossed arms, tightly compressed lips, or raised eyebrows. Take these as a cue to follow up with Janie, who may be using this discussion as an opportunity to get in the last word on a previous fight. Was there a specific situation in which they were late to dinner at her parents' house? What happened? What did she feel in that situation, and how did she communicate it to Lance? If she's referring to an isolated incident, you can coach her to express her annoyance or frustration in a way that would help Lance hear and understand it.

But even if the difficulty is an ongoing one, remind Janie that the goal is for her to help Lance understand her mother, and do so in a way that strengthens the marital partnership. Simply telling Lance what to do won't accomplish this. Coach her to congruently and constructively send a message that communicates: "My mother is important to me, and you're important to me. That's why I would love for you to understand her better." Once she gets this message across in a way that doesn't trigger Lance's defensiveness, she may need to listen to a response from him. When they both feel heard, they can return to a discussion of practical strategies for getting along.

In coaching this discussion, keep the couple focused on building a positive relationship with their respective in-laws with each other's active support. Use listening skills to promote the exploration of unspoken expectations, and help partners move to specific recommendations based on their own experience. Framing the conversation as a spiritual matter of honoring parents can help couples take a more active than reactive stance, which also helps them invest positively in their identity as a couple.

A word of caution: in some cases, one or both sets of parents are overly intrusive, and the partners agree that this is a problem. Consider using the decision-making process described in chapter 5 to help them develop appropriate boundaries. Defining limits in this way can help a couple affirm their own needs while still staying connected to extended family. If you suspect that actual physical or psychological abuse is involved, consider a referral to a qualified therapist who can give the couple the deeper and longer-term support they may need to establish clear boundaries.

A conversation about questions 5 and 6 may already reveal implicit parental expectations. If not, question 7 (see page 123) will bring at least one expectation from each family to light. These expectations may have been explicitly stated by the parents or only perceived by the partners. Sharing and discussing these will help couples anticipate issues that may shape the couple's extended family relationships going forward.

In coaching this discussion, invite each partner to take turns sharing the expectation that he or she named. You can also prompt the couple to share a story illustrating how these expectations have played out in their respective families. This is particularly important in the case of unspoken expectations, since it's possible that certain parental behaviors have been misinterpreted; in other words, ask what leads them to believe that their parents have this expectation. Encourage partners to also reflect on the importance of such unspoken expectations and why they have not been voiced. Your task as coach is to encourage the couple to use constructive communication to build a shared understanding of their extended family context, and a jointly owned approach to responding to expectations as a couple.

In some cases, the influence of the parental expectations discussed can already be seen in the process of wedding planning, as parents have made their wishes known regarding the venue, guest list, and the like. You can ask the couple to forecast how these expectations or others like them may arise at another time in their future, such as when the couple must move for a new job, have children, or must care for aging parents. The point, of course, is not to predict the future in such a way as to have the illusion of controlling it, but rather to practice having relationship-affirming conversations about how they will face expectations together.

A conversation about extended family relationships and expectations can easily become a defensive discussion of the demands and difficulties couples will face. In the final question, we invite couples not only to name what they believe the biggest area of tension will be, but also to consider what blessing might come of their union. Some partners have had such a positive experience of each other's families that naming just one blessing will be difficult. For others, coming up with one may be the challenge.

In coaching this conversation, try to orient the couple toward the hope implied in the question. Chances are that the tensions they name will be more concrete than the blessings—if indeed any blessings are named! Be curious. Wonder aloud how the blessing might actually look in practice, and what it might take to turn tensions into blessings. If partners are unable to identify a blessing, given their negative family experiences, ask them instead to identify a blessing *they* would like to bring their new extended family. Then ask them to discuss what they could do now, and after they're married, to become the people who will be the kind of blessing to others that they envision.

In that vein, you can also consider together how the blessings they've named or envisioned could be used to honor their parents on their wedding day. Who walks the bride down the aisle? The father? Both parents? The whole extended family? How else are parents and family members involved in the ceremony or reception? Such decisions can be freighted with symbolic meaning for the family. Help couples be intentional about communicating the positive meanings they *want* to communicate, so that they can begin learning how to be a blessing to their family together as a couple.

Additional Resources

- **Book:** Gary Chapman, *Things I Wish I'd Known Before We Got Married* (Chicago: Northfield Publishing, 2010).

  A brief, highly readable book for engaged couples, with discussion questions at the end of each of its twelve chapters. Chapter 10 introduces five "key issues" for couples to consider with respect to extended family, including holidays, traditions, and expectations.

•**Book:** Susan Forward, *Toxic In-Laws* (New York: HarperCollins, 2001).

Written for couples who are experiencing difficulties with intrusive and disrespectful in-laws, using real case studies to give practical recommendations about boundaries and communication. The book is best for engaged couples whose relationships with in-laws are already negative, or for those who can learn from the suggestions without overreacting to parental demands.

Chapter Twelve

Religious Devotion and Practice

It's been said that "the family that prays together stays together."[1] Families of many faiths—not just Christians—find shared religious rituals to be an important source of unity.[2] Indeed, sociological evidence suggests that religiousness, and specifically a *similarity* of religious beliefs and practices between spouses, can benefit the marriage relationship.[3] The converse, unfortunately, can also be true: religious *differences* can be the source of *dis*-unity.

Several books, for example, have been written for the believing wives of unbelieving husbands, telling poignantly of the frustration and resentment that arises on both sides of the spiritual gap.[4] But this isn't just a matter of Christians (or the pastors who marry them!) heedlessly ignoring Paul's command to not be "unequally yoked" (2 Cor. 6:14, KJV). Lee and Leslie Strobel, for example, began their marriage as an atheist and an agnostic who were very much in love. They enjoyed their early years of marriage—until Leslie became a Christian. Little by little, Lee began to resent the feeling that Jesus and the church had come between them.[5]

A mentor helped coach Leslie to be a consistently loving, humble, and supportive wife along the lines of 1 Peter 3:1-2. But her growing faith unavoidably upset the apple cart in countless ways. Her values began to change about how to spend money. Her new churchgoing habit threatened his Sunday morning routine. As their children began to attend Sunday school, Lee worried that he would be the odd man out and that the kids would begin thinking of him as an evangelism project instead of respecting him as their father. Eventually, though, Leslie's patient persistence paid off; her faithful example of Christlikeness was the means by which the Holy Spirit opened Lee's heart to the gospel.[6] Not all such stories have a happy ending, of course; changes may take years, if they happen at all.[7]

But spiritual mismatches aren't just between Christians and non-Christians. There can also be marital tension between two believers when their spiritual practices and levels of devotion don't line up. Gary Chapman, for example, tells the story of newlyweds Jill and Matt, who came to see him with a problem. Here's how Jill framed it:

> Matt doesn't want to go to church with me anymore. He says that church is boring and that he feels closer to God on the golf course than he does in the church. So for the last month, he drives off to the golf course while I drive off to church . . . Before we got married, Matt went to church with me every Sunday. He always seemed to like it. . . . He told me that he was a Christian, but how can you be a Christian and not want to go to church? He says that I'm judging him and maybe I am. But I'm deeply hurt and I'm beginning to feel that maybe we made a mistake by getting married.[8]

There are men who will fake spirituality to win a wife, and then ditch the act sometime after the wedding. But that's not the case here. Matt didn't grow up in the church; he became a Christian only in college. He went to church with Jill because he found it interesting, and she took this for a deeper level of commitment than he really had. When it was no longer interesting, he simply stopped going, and couldn't understand why she felt so deeply betrayed.

Christians share "one Lord, one faith, one baptism" (Eph. 4:5), yet are also taught that they have different gifts by one and the same Holy Spirit (1 Cor. 12:4-11). There is, in other words, an intrinsic and creative tension in the church between unity and diversity that serves God's purposes. But unless a congregation is also characterized by deep humility, that tension can dissolve into contentious competition.

Something similar is true when two people bring their spiritual differences into marriage and pledge their oneness as a couple. It's one thing to accept the variety of beliefs and behaviors they witness each Sunday, but it's another to live every day with those same beliefs and behaviors in their husbands and wives. Moreover, when a spiritual gap causes friction between spouses, the resulting conflict can easily affect their spiritual lives in turn (e.g., 1 Pet. 3:7). Spouses get testy and defensive, looking for the worst in each other—and frequently finding it! Such cycles of negativity are toxic to their faith and marriage both.

Conversations about religious practices and devotion present both an opportunity and a challenge. As the Strobels have written: "Marriage relationships are deepened when we have meaningful conversations about matters of real substance. Intimacy grows the more we delve into each other's world. . . . [S]o why should our spirituality be off-limits? . . . [But the] truth is that most people have never really formulated strong beliefs about spiritual matters."[9] Thus, some couples come to marriage unsure of what they believe or why, and even less certain about each other's commitments. Using their responses to the Conversation Jumpstarter, encourage them to appreciate what they share in common, while also exploring their differences. Here are the areas for discussion.

Religious Activity

Hundreds of studies have been done over the years, essentially asking whether religion is "good for you," and if so, how. Many of these studies are based on large-scale surveys, where virtually the only measure of religiousness is how often people attend religious services of some kind. Critics scoff that this is a poor measure of the depth and richness of a person's actual faith. As evangelist Billy Sunday famously wrote, "Going to church doesn't make you a Christian, any more than going to a garage makes you an automobile."[10] The point is well taken. Still, wouldn't you hope that people who consistently spent time in local congregations would be affected in some positive way?

Evidence suggests that this may be the case. Researchers have found that couples who attend services more frequently, particularly if they do so together, have stronger marriages and are less likely to divorce.[11] In fact, in one study, how often people attended religious services was a better predictor of marital fidelity than how close they felt to God or how often they prayed.[12] It's not because going to church makes you a Christian! But going to church together seems to say something important about how the spouses view God and the marriage both.

That's why this section of the Jumpstarter begins by helping couples identify and discuss their expectations about religious behavior. Don't think of it as an assessment of their religiousness, but as an easier way to start a conversation about the beliefs and values that make these behaviors significant.

Question 1 (see page 124) uses some of the most common indicators of religiousness to get a quick read of each person's behavior. The point is not to make judgments about who's more religious, but rather to look for important differences between the spouses-to-be. One partner, for example, may know that the other goes to church regularly but be distressed to find out that he or she never reads the Bible.

This discussion leads into question 2 (see page 124), which brings relationship expectations to the fore. For example, in the case mentioned earlier, Jill had a clear expectation that Matt would go to church with her. But many couples will not have given this much thought, having instead some vague idea that if they're both Christians, they'll just somehow "be Christian together."

If there is open disagreement in their responses to question 2, you may have to work at keeping people calm and helping them to listen attentively. Again, they should try their best to understand, even if they still disagree. But you should also look for signs of apathy or capitulation. For example, she leans forward and says, "I really want us to go to church together every week." He shrugs, looks down at the ground, and says flatly, "I guess. If you really want to." Left at that, the likelihood is that he will try to do what she wants, but only for a time.

Here, it would help to focus on the process, not just the content; an exchange like that is likely to leave both of them feeling frustrated. As we've suggested before, comment not just on *what* was said, but also on *how* it was said: "Jill, it sounds like going to church together is really important to you. And Matt, I get that you want to make Jill happy, but you don't sound too excited about this whole church thing. Is that right? Can you talk to each other about why this is so important to you, Jill, and Matt, what your reservations are?" Keep the conversation between *them* if you can, and resist the impulse to teach them why church is important, unless they ask.

Religious Values

As suggested earlier, we don't believe that Christian faith can be reduced down to religious behavior. The teaching of Jesus (e.g., Matt. 6:1-8; 24:23-28) is definitive: what matters is not simply the acts of piety that others see, but the state of the heart that only God sees.

But that doesn't mean that religious behavior is unimportant, only that no amount of being religious can reconcile us to God (Eph. 2:8-9). As the Apostle James insists, one can't claim to be faithful if there is no practical evidence of that faith in a person's behavior (James 2:14-17). As a pastor, you don't just try to stuff Christian "head knowledge" into people; you want their lives to be transformed as they grow in likeness to Jesus (e.g., 2 Cor. 3:18; Eph. 4:11-13; Col. 1:28). What Christians believe and profess must express who they truly are, or are becoming.

There can be a discrepancy not only in terms of how people practice their faith, but also in terms of how important the practices are to them personally. One person reads the Bible as if it were a requirement to be checked off a list. Another would no more skip the daily reading than a hungry person would skip a meal. What if these two people married each other? How much a spiritual mismatch between prospective spouses matters depends in part on how deeply they value their spiritual commitments.

Question 3 (see page 124) asks how much their religious beliefs actually guide what they do in daily life. The full range of possible responses is given, including the option that they don't consider themselves to have any religious beliefs at all. Most people will choose one of the middle three responses; when they do, they're asked to provide a concrete example of a particular decision or action that was guided by their beliefs. It's one thing to say in an offhand way that one's beliefs truly matter; it's another to show how.

Again, this is not intended as a measure of religiousness, but rather as an opportunity to reflect honestly about themselves and to learn about each other. Start by looking for discrepancies in their responses to the first part of the question. The answers themselves may be ambiguous. He may say "a little" out of genuine humility, wishing he could give a different response. She may say "everything" but mean it more as a reflection of the person she is *trying* to be, rather than the person she believes she truly *is* at that moment.

Use their answers to the second part to further the discussion. An answer may be vague; for example, the connection between a stated value and a particular decision may be unclear. If so, watch for signs of puzzlement in the other partner, and allow him or her to voice his or her own curiosity. If he or she doesn't, make an observation:

"Michelle, you look puzzled by what Paul said." If she nods, you can follow with: "Tell him what puzzles you." Alternatively, you can voice your own confusion: "Paul, I'm not sure I follow what you wrote here."

On the positive side, you may get a story that demonstrates a clear willingness to make sacrifices for what one believes. Encourage them to affirm what they admire in each other: "Paul, you had that 'Wow!' look on your face just now as Michelle was talking. What did that story tell you about her?" Sharing their admiration for each other's faith-filled decisions and actions is a good way of both strengthening their bond and encouraging further faithfulness.

Raising Children and Family-of-Origin Influences

Lynn Donovan, writing about her marriage to a non-Christian husband, tells of how deeply she longed for her daughter to go to a faith-based school. She had always had the primary responsibility for child-care decisions and so assumed that this too would be largely her choice. But when she broached the subject with her husband, he flatly refused. She tried every clever argument she could think of, but to no avail. Her husband was adamant. Their daughter would go to public, not private, school, period.[13]

Her story illustrates what often seems true of spiritually misaligned couples: tacit agreements about how to handle religious differences take on special significance when children are involved. For some couples at the premarital stage, this may seem like a distant and relatively unimportant concern. But others hail from families with over-my-dead-body convictions, families who might actually say, "No grandchild of ours is going to be raised _____" (fill in the despised denomination of your choice). For such reasons, the Jumpstarter folds this potentially sensitive discussion into the larger context of family-of-origin influences.

Either partner may envision some religious upbringing for their children. Instead of asking for the name of a particular tradition, question 5 (see page 125) asks for expectations to be put in operational terms: what activities do you want your kids to participate in? Church? Sunday school? Family devotions? Listen for differences not just in the content of their answers, but also in their intensity. "Oh, I don't know. I guess it would be nice if the kids went to church with us," is different from, "The kids are going to church with us every Sunday whether they like it or not." Make an observation: "Claire, this sounds really important to you, but Cliff, it sounds like it doesn't matter much to you at all." Help them to express why it is or isn't important, and to listen carefully to each other.

Notice, however, that question 5 is also sandwiched between two family-of-origin questions. Each partner will have answered the questions and read each other's responses in this order. This is intentional. We want both partners to begin thinking about how their expectations for their children are shaped by their own experiences of the past. This shifts the footing of the discussion. Left to themselves, they can easily slide from discussing differences into arguing about whose expectations are right or wrong. But using their answers to questions 4 and 6 (see page 125), you can help them explore where their expectations come from, and what it is that they are trying to preserve or avoid as they build a new marriage. At this point, understanding each other's values and expectations is a higher priority than coming to some agreement about what to do.

Adopt this same stance in the way you manage the discussion. The bride may have been raised in a spiritually abusive congregation; her parents were deeply wounded and have never returned to the church. She identifies herself as a Christian but is understandably leery of local congregations. The groom, however, remembers his home church as a warm extended family.

Take the pressure off; they don't have to resolve their differences right away. Instead, they can focus on listening to each other's stories. Toward that end, help the partners to explore and be curious about their own and each other's responses. Ask them: What's special or meaningful about the family rituals they remember? What was experienced as oppressive or inappropriate? How were their experiences different? What would change if they were to see spirituality and religion through each other's eyes? The more they are able to understand and empathize with each other here and now, the easier and less divisive their conversations about their children's religious training will be.

A Final Note

We realize that this chapter may conflict with how you understand your pastoral role in a way that none of the other chapters do. It's one thing to help couples discuss who will take out the garbage. It's another to sit quietly and calmly while they discuss whether they want to have anything to do with the church.

Perhaps you've known the bride since she was in diapers. She's marrying a man she fell in love with in college. He says he's open to the faith but is decidedly lukewarm and not shy of saying so. She's not fazed by this at all but firmly believes that given time she can talk him into it, and all will be well. What do you do? Take her aside for a little private pastoral guidance?

There are, of course, no simple answers. And we're not asking you to set aside your authoritative role as a minister of the gospel. But as we said all the way back in chapter 1, premarital preparation is not pastoral counseling, and working with couples is different from working with individuals. You may want to pull the bride aside out of your pastoral concern for her, but in so doing, you have compromised your pastoral commitment to *him*. In other words, in premarital work, your job, as far as conscience allows, is to be an advocate for the *relationship*. If at some point, you feel you can no longer do that, you should let them both know and recuse yourself from the process. That's why it's important to be clear up front, during the orientation session, about what your policies are. It is to that final consideration that we turn in the epilogue.

Additional Resources

•**Book:** Lee and Leslie Strobel, *Surviving a Spiritual Mismatch in Marriage* (Grand Rapids: Zondervan, 2002).

This book, cited earlier in the chapter, was written primarily for women. However, unlike similar titles listed in the footnotes, the husband and wife wrote this one together. Other notable features include chapters on "dating traps" and spiritual mismatches between Christians; prayer and application/discussion guides; and an open letter from Lee Strobel that a wife can photocopy and then give to her unbelieving husband.

The Big Picture

We hope you'll find this book to be a useful and practical ministry resource. Although we've suggested a particular strategy for using it, we've designed it to be flexible and modular. Use it in the way that best supports your ministry.

We want to circle back to the story we told at the beginning and the fact that even people who don't know you may ask you to perform their wedding. But they might be surprised or even resistant if you say, as we would, that you expect them to participate in some kind of preparation process first. What if there isn't enough time? Do you politely turn them down, or do the wedding anyway? More generally, do you make premarital preparation a requirement for all couples, or just offer it as an option for those who want it?

We're not going to insist that everybody have the same policy. We know that some pastors figure, "If I don't do the wedding, they'll get someone else anyway. At least if I do it, I can have *some* positive influence." Possibly. That's an on-the-spot ministry decision, like so many others in which you have to balance situational factors against your larger goals.

We do, however, want to keep those larger goals in front of you. The question is, where should you draw a line, and why? Some who work with engaged couples insist on a specific premarital regimen that must be completed well before the actual wedding date. Others may draw much less of a line, or no line at all, taking all comers and adjusting their practices from situation to situation.

Rather than advocate for a specific policy, we simply suggest that you take a stand *somewhere* and be crystal clear as to why. As we've said, one reason for putting a deadline on completing the preparation process is to leave the door open for the couple to delay or even call off the wedding. The fact is that the closer they get to the actual wedding date, the harder it becomes to pull the plug. The venue has been booked and a deposit paid; the invitations have been sent and people have begun to RSVP; family members have made travel arrangements. Even if they begin to have serious misgivings about getting married, it may feel much too complicated and embarrassing to back out. That would indeed be an unfortunate consequence of not having set some simple limits on the process beforehand.

So if you don't already have some policy about premarital preparation, decide on one now, before the next couple calls. What will be your requirements for the process? Are you willing to officiate a wedding if there's been no preparation? If yes, then under what conditions, if any? Set some boundaries; you can always make an exception if it seems wise or necessary. If you think it may be awkward to establish such boundaries when actually speaking with a couple, then work out in advance what you would say in different situations, or put it in writing.

If you're not sure you can commit up front to marrying a couple, you can still help them prepare for marriage while you temporarily leave your agreement to officiate open-ended. But have compassion for the stress of wedding planning. At some point the couple will need a firm commitment from you, and the sooner the better. If it seems there won't be enough time for them to find another minister, it would be better to simply decline from the start.

Keep the big picture in mind. Policy decisions should be shaped by larger considerations; where you stand depends on what you want to stand *for*, as a leader in your congregation and community, and as one whose ministry represents the healing and restoring work of God. Your policy should reflect what you wish to communicate about what's important, both to your church and the world. Here are some questions to consider. First: **What do you want your commitment to premarital work to say about marriage itself?**

Requiring couples to take their union seriously by spending time and energy preparing for it should send an important message: marriage is too precious in God's sight to be entered lightly. The wedding is but a moment; the marriage, hopefully, is for life. It's both sad and ironic that couples, their families, and even their churches put so much emphasis on the former and give so little attention to the latter.

As a pastor, why do *you* believe marriage is important? What's your reason for helping prepare couples to succeed at it? Being clear and articulate on this point is the prerequisite to forming policies that express that personal commitment. Those policies, in turn, will help communicate your values regarding the importance of strong marriages.

More than that, you can ask yourself what else you can do in your ministry to embody and teach those values. For example, having helped prepare a couple for marriage, what will you say at their wedding? Will the guests leave the ceremony with their hope grounded in the power of romance and "true love" or in the steadfast mercy of God?

We said at the outset that we would not be saying much about a theology of marriage, narrowing our focus to the pragmatics of marriage preparation. Throughout the book, however, we've made relevant statements of Christian belief. In chapter 2, for example, we pointed to the way in which people's search for the one soul mate who would "complete" them is a form of idolatry. That's not something that you're likely to slip into one of your sessions. But it can be taught from the pulpit as a way of helping the members of your church family to put Romans 12:2 into practice: "Do not conform to the pattern of this world, but be transformed by the renewing of your mind. Then you will be able to test and approve what God's will is—his good, pleasing and perfect will." In this case, "approving God's will" would mean wanting what God wants for marriage: not a soul mate but an intimate brother or sister in Christ who knows what it means to be part of one body in the 24/7 of life together. Imagine the difference if everyone who came through the preparation process already understood this!

So, how will marriage preparation relate to your larger teaching ministry, and what do both say about God's will for marriage? This leads naturally to the second question: *How do you want premarital preparation to be related to the larger vision and mission of your congregation?*

The only thing some churches do for couples is host weddings, while others demonstrate a far more robust commitment to marriage. There's a shared sense of mission, which is concretely demonstrated through sermons, retreats, workshops, conferences, or small group ministries. The more public your church's dedication to strengthening marriage, the less people will perceive your premarital policies as merely idiosyncratic, as just "the pastor's thing."

If you are personally committed to helping couples prepare for marriage, how will you communicate that commitment to the congregation? How much do you want them to share that commitment? As you frame policy, consider not only your own beliefs but also how you see this ministry relating to the larger mission of your church. If you can't successfully articulate that to the congregation, then either the ministry or the mission may need to be rethought!

Third: *How do you want your ministry to coordinate with what others may be doing for marriage in your community?* The more you approach premarital preparation with a missional mind-set, the more you'll be compelled to think beyond the boundaries of your congregation to your local community. At one level, it can be as simple as scouting out existing resources. Who in your community offers communication workshops? Where can you find a financial planning expert or a marriage counselor? How can you partner with them in a way that enhances both your mission and theirs?

At another level, though, is the question of working to create a shared sense of mission across the community itself. What could happen if all the key players involved in wedding planning in a given community took a common stance promoting healthy marriage?

Let's face it: these days, the three major factors in many engaged couples' choice of a wedding venue are location, location, and location. The couple's relationship with a pastor or congregation often matters less than how the sanctuary would look in wedding photos. (We know of one family who hired professional models to be the wedding party!) Couples shop venues, encountering a variety of policies and prices. And some shop pastors, too; the requirement of having to attend several sessions of premarital preparation may be a deterrent when they can find easier pickings else-where. But what if every pastor of every church in a particular community had the same policy?[1]

With whom can you partner to make an impact upon marriage throughout the community, and how might that partnership look? It may mean working to form a coalition of like-minded pastors who strategize together. It may mean networking with other professionals in the community. Think outside the congregational box. Take someone to lunch and start a conversation. Do some vision casting, and see what happens.

Finally: ***How will your ministry of premarital preparation help embody God's ongoing work of restoration?*** This, of course, is the biggest picture of all, yet one that supports and pervades all the others. It's possible to have premarital prepara-tion be just one more freestanding thing on the ministry menu. We hope, however, that the very reason you're reading this book is because you have a broader vision of the importance of healthy marriage relationships, whether to society at large or to the life of your congregation. You want to make sure that the couples who come under your pastoral wing have the best chance you can give them at creating a godly and successful union. And you want this because you believe God wants it.

We have no illusions that the simple process we've described in these pages will save every couple from divorce or even bitter disagreement. None of us can unilater-ally save couples from their own folly. But something can still be done. In the days and weeks before a wedding, you have a unique opportunity to cast a vision for what marriage can be. In the preparation process, your part is to give couples a fighting chance in the midst of a sin-stained culture that is frequently unfriendly to marriage. They need a glimmer of realistic hope that despite their differences they can learn to work together—that two really can become one. When you walk them successfully through difficult conversations, you give them that hope.

Ultimately, in its own small way, that hope can be the embodiment of our bibli-cal hope: that however much we must all groan in the present, God is at work liber-ating his creation from decay while we await the fullness of our redemption (Rom. 8:18-25).

There are no ideal couples, just those who are more or less broken and vulner-able in their own ways. That's the reality within which all ministry necessarily resides. In love, you work for the good of the couples who come to you, knowing that what-ever redemptive purpose your ministry might serve, it's always God's work first before it can be your own.

Soli Deo gloria. Welcome to the adventure.

—Cameron and Jim

Appendix A

The Conversation Jumpstarter

Important: Please read these instructions before you begin!

My name:_____

The Conversation Jumpstarter (CJ) is a tool your pastor/coach will use to help prepare you for marriage. The CJ will ask you to answer questions in six important areas of relationship that often pose a challenge to married couples: roles, love and affection, money, parenting, in-laws, and spirituality. Some of the questions will be easy to answer; others will be more difficult.

Don't discuss your answers with your partner until your coach instructs you to do so.

Answer the questions as honestly as you can. This is not a test, and there are no right or wrong answers. The purpose of the CJ is to help you have candid conversations with your fiancé or fiancée about important things, so be as honest as possible.

Take your time. Don't rush through it. Make time to do this well. We recommend the following: read one section (e.g., on roles), and then put it aside without answering it. Come back later (you can even sleep on it!) when you have at least thirty minutes to fill it out. Do one section a day until the whole CJ is complete.

Some questions ask for personal information and provide a place for you to write in your answers. If you have to use additional sheets of paper, be sure to staple them to the appropriate section of the CJ.

Several of the questions ask you to make a choice between options. In each case, just check (✓) the option that sounds the most like what you currently do or believe. If you don't like any of the options, feel free to write in your own!

Your pastor/coach will tell you what to do with the CJ and your responses when you've finished. We hope that this tool will help you learn something about yourself and about each other!

SECTION 1: ROLES AND RESPONSIBILITIES

1.   Think about the regular responsibilities each member of your family had in your home when you were growing up. Here are just a few, to jog your memory:

- *Food/meals:* plan meals; shop for groceries; cook; set/clear the table; wash dishes (load dishwasher); dry/put dishes away
- *Laundry:* wash clothes; dry; iron; sort; fold; hang/put away
- *Indoor maintenance:* dust; vacuum; mop; clean the bathroom; clean the kitchen; take out garbage; make beds; tidy/neaten; organize; water plants
- *Outdoor maintenance:* mow; weed; water; rake; shovel snow; wash windows; wash cars
- *Mechanical:* fix/replace things that aren't working; maintain cars
- *Pets:* feed; walk; bathe; clean up after; take to vet

a. What household responsibilities did *you* have? (Feel free to add to the list as needed.) How often did you have to do them?

b. Which ones did you *dislike* the most? What was it about them that you didn't like?

c. Which ones did you *like* the most? What was it about them that you liked?

d. What household responsibilities did your *mother* have? How often did she have to do them?

e. What household responsibilities did your *father* have? How often did he have to do them?

2. Thinking about your upcoming marriage, what responsibilities do you envision for yourself? For your spouse? And what responsibilities, honestly, would you rather avoid?

3. Describe who contributed to the family income as you were growing up. Who worked outside the home? Was that work full-time or part-time? How was that work perceived in the family—as a career, a way to make extra money, or something else?

4. Write down two or three hopes and dreams you have regarding your own work or career, and how you would want your partner to support you in the pursuit of those dreams.

5. Couples can get so busy with work that they forget to take time to nurture their marriage. What do you think the warning signs would be if this were to happen in *your* relationship? What's one thing you could personally commit to now, to help prevent that from happening?

SECTION 2: LOVE AND AFFECTION

1. Thinking about your parents when you were growing up, which of the following best describes how they showed physical affection?

    ❏ "Cold as ice"   ❏ "Polite and proper"

    ❏ "Top secret"   ❏ "Comfortably close"

    ❏ "Distant and diplomatic"   ❏ "Too hot to handle"

Think of a brief story that best illustrates how your parents expressed affection, and summarize it here:

2. Which of the following best describes how you and your partner feel about the physical affection in your relationship? In the first column, answer for yourself; in the second column, check what you think your *partner* would say.

I would say that the expression of   *My partner* would say that the expression
physical affection in our relationship . . .   of physical affection in our relationship . . .

    ❏ Desperately needs attention   ❏ Desperately needs attention

    ❏ Needs some attention   ❏ Needs some attention

    ❏ Is just about right   ❏ Is just about right

    ❏ Meets my needs   ❏ Meets his or her needs

    ❏ Is exactly what I want   ❏ Is exactly what he or she wants

3. Think about the ways you express physical affection with your partner that you *most* enjoy and those you *least* enjoy. Answer these questions:

What do you do to let your partner know what you enjoy and why you enjoy it?

What do you do to let your partner know what you *do not* enjoy?

If you had one request or one suggestion for improving how you as a couple express affection, what would that be?

4.   Physical affection is a common way couples experience intimacy. Use an X to mark how important physical affection is to you in knowing that you are special and loved in this relationship. Use an 0 to mark how important you think physical affection is to your partner.

|——————————————————————————————————|

     Not important   Extremely

        at all   important

Now assume you are married. Use the same marks to indicate how important you think your *sexual relationship* will be both to you and to your partner in feeling special and loved. Use an X for yourself, and an 0 for your partner.

|——————————————————————————————————|

     Not important   Extremely

        at all   important

5.   If you were to list one or two worries or concerns about your wedding night in particular, or your sexual relationship in general, what would it or they be?

6.   Please answer the following questions regarding your plans for birth control.

Which statement best describes
your plan for birth control?

❑ We have no plans.
❑ I have some worries about the plan.
❑ The plan was a compromise.

❑ We have a good plan.
❑ I am fully confident in our plan.

How satisfied are you with the way you
made this decision as a couple?

❑ Very dissatisfied
❑ Dissatisfied
❑ Uncertain (mixed
   feelings)
❑ Satisfied
❑ Very satisfied

7.   It's not uncommon for spouses to have feelings of romantic or sexual interest in someone other than their partner. Has this ever happened to you? What did you do to handle this? How would you want your partner to handle a similar situation?

SECTION 3: MONEY

1. In each group below, check the option that sounds more like you. Do you typically . . .

    ❑ spend more money to get something nice? Or
    ❑ spend less money to get something that's good enough?

    ❑ spend reasonably but freely, without having to keep track? Or
    ❑ budget carefully, to keep your spending within specific limits?

    ❑ pay the bills, buy what you want, and *then* set aside what's left? Or
    ❑ pay the bills, set some money aside, and *then* spend what's left?

    ❑ use credit cards to get things you want, as long as you can afford the monthly payment? Or
    ❑ use credit cards only as long as you can pay off the balance each month? Or
    ❑ use credit cards only in emergencies? Or
    ❑ not use credit cards at all?

2. How would you like money to be handled in your marriage? Check one option in each group.

    ❑ I should be free to decide how to spend the money I earn.
    ❑ I should be free to decide how to spend the money I earn, within agreed limits.
    ❑ The money I earn goes into a common pot, and both of us can spend it within agreed limits.
    ❑ The money I earn goes into a common pot, and both of us can spend it as we choose.
    ❑ All of our money should go into joint accounts.
    ❑ All of our money should go into individual accounts.
    ❑ Some of our money should go into joint accounts and some into individual accounts.
    ❑ All of our money should go into joint accounts, with a mutual understanding of what expenditures need to be checked with each other first.

3. What is your current monthly income (gross and net)?

    Gross (before taxes) monthly income: $_____ *Net (after taxes):* $_____

4.   What is your current debt? Take into account any money owed to anyone, including mortgages, credit card balances, student loans, unpaid bills, loans from friends or family members, and so on.

Total amount of debt / money owed: $_____

5.   How much are you currently paying per month to service these debts?

Total monthly debt payments: $_____

6.   If you know anything about how your parents managed money and debt in your family while you were growing up, what did you like or dislike about what they did? Write down examples to illustrate these things. Think about which aspects you want to have continue into your upcoming marriage, and which you would rather change or avoid; write these down as well.

7.   Dream a little: what goal would you pursue right now, if money were no object? What would you buy; where would you go; what would you be? What dream do you have for the future that you would want your spouse to support?

SECTION 4: PARENTING

(Note: the wording of the questions below assumes that some couples are remarrying and possibly bringing children into the marriage.)

1.   In the space below, make a list of all your *brothers and sisters*, by name, from oldest to youngest, *including yourself.* Put an asterisk (*) next to the names of your biological siblings.

2.   In the space below, make a list of all your *children* (if any) from previous relationships. Write their names and ages.

3.   Would you rather . . .

   ❑ begin having children together as soon as possible? Or
   ❑ begin having children soon, but take a little time to just be a couple first? Or
   ❑ not think yet about having children? Or
   ❑ adopt children? Or
   ❑ not have children at all? (Check this response if you are bringing children into the marriage and would prefer not to have any more children together.)

4.   Complete the following sentence by putting a tentative number in the blank:

"As I think about the future, I imagine us as a couple with _____ kids."

5.   If you have children from a previous relationship, who had the primary responsibility for dealing with their misbehavior? (If you don't have children yet, skip to the next question.)

   ❑ I did.
   ❑ My spouse / the other parent did.
   ❑ We dealt with it equally or together.
   ❑ We seldom dealt with misbehavior.

6.   As you anticipate your upcoming marriage, who will have the primary responsibility for dealing with misbehavior in your new family?

❏ Me
❏ My spouse
❏ We will deal with it equally or together.
❏ There will be no children in the family.

7.   Growing up in your family, which parent did you feel closer to emotionally?

❏ Mom
❏ Dad
❏ I felt close to both of them.
❏ I didn't feel close to either of them.
❏ Other adult (explain:_____)

8.   Think about how your parents responded when you misbehaved as a child. Who was the primary disciplinarian? Was there too much or too little discipline? Was it harsh or lenient, predictable or unpredictable? Write out some examples below. In general, in what ways would you (or do you, if you already have children) model your own parenting on how your parents treated you? What should be kept the same, and what should be different? Write these thoughts down as well.

SECTION 5: IN-LAWS AND EXTENDED FAMILY RELATIONSHIPS

1.   Think about how your own parents seem to feel about your upcoming marriage. Then look at the following sentence, and put a check by the phrase that best completes it:

"Overall, when it comes to our getting married, my parents are . . ."
   ❏ Very supportive
   ❏ Somewhat supportive
   ❏ Indifferent
   ❏ Somewhat concerned
   ❏ Very concerned

2.   Now do the same for how you think your *partner's* parents feel about your upcoming marriage. Put a check by the phrase that best completes the sentence below:

"Overall, when it comes to our getting married, my partner's parents are . . ."
   ❏ Very supportive
   ❏ Somewhat supportive
   ❏ Indifferent
   ❏ Somewhat concerned
   ❏ Very concerned

3.   Couples often turn to their parents for various forms of support. If you needed it, how likely would you be personally to go to your own parents for either emotional or financial support? Check one answer in each column.

Emotional support
   ❏ Very likely
   ❏ Somewhat likely
   ❏ Not very likely
   ❏ Not likely at all

Financial support
   ❏ Very likely
   ❏ Somewhat likely
   ❏ Not very likely
   ❏ Not likely at all

4.   Sometimes, it goes the other way: parents turn to their children for support. If they needed it, how likely would your parents be to come to you for either emotional or financial support? Check one answer in each column.

Emotional support
- ❏ Very likely
- ❏ Somewhat likely
- ❏ Not very likely
- ❏ Not likely at all

Financial support
- ❏ Very likely
- ❏ Somewhat likely
- ❏ Not very likely
- ❏ Not likely at all

5.   If you were to give your partner one piece of advice to help him or her to understand or get along better with your **mother**, what would that be?

6.   If you were to give your partner one piece of advice to help him or her to understand or get along better with your **father**, what would that be?

7.   Name one expectation that your own parents will have for the two of you as a couple. Is this a spoken or an unspoken expectation?

8.   What do you think will be the biggest tension in relating to your future in-laws? What do you hope will be the biggest blessing?

- The biggest tension will be . . .

- The biggest blessing will be . . .

SECTION 6: SPIRITUALITY AND DEVOTION

1.   Approximately how often do you do each of the following? Check one response for each line.

	Never	Seldom	Once a month	Once a week	Every day
Go to church or religious service . . . . ❏	❏	❏	❏	❏
Read the Bible or other sacred texts by yourself. . . . . ❏	❏	❏	❏	❏
Read other religious materials (books, magazines, blogs, etc.) . . . . ❏	❏	❏	❏	❏
Pray to God by yourself. . . . . ❏	❏	❏	❏	❏

2.   What religious activities, if any, do you hope the two of you will do on a regular basis, together as a couple? Name them in the space below (if none, write "none").

3.   How much would you say your spiritual and/or religious beliefs and values guide your decisions and behavior in daily life (e.g., how you spend money, how you relate to other people, etc.)?

❏ Not at all
❏ A little; occasionally
❏ A lot
❏ They guide everything I do.
❏ I don't think of myself as having spiritual or religious beliefs.

If you answered "a little," "a lot," or "they guide everything I do," then in the space below please give a brief example of how a decision you've made and/or an action you took was guided by your beliefs/values.

4.   In what religious or spiritual tradition were you raised, if any? Name and describe it below.

5.   If you have children, in what organized religious activities, if any, do you want them to participate? In what religious family activities? Name and describe them below. (If you already have kids, describe what you have already done, and what you would like to have continue.)

6.   Think about the religious and spiritual commitments of your family when you were growing up, and how they relate to your upcoming marriage. Looking back, what beliefs and behaviors did your parents try to pass on to you? What weekly or annual religious rituals did you do together? What part of these or other traditions would your parents want you to bring into your marriage? What would *you* like to keep the same in your marriage, and what would you like to change?

Appendix B

Constructive Communication

My name:_____

<u>Calm down</u> before having or continuing difficult discussions.

- When I'm stressed out, my body gives me these **warning signs:**

_____   _____   _____

- Four rules for **taking a break:**

    1. Either of us can ask for one.
    2. We should commit to a time and place to try again.
    3. It should be at least twenty minutes long.
    4. During the break, we should only do things that help us calm down.

<u>Listen</u> in a way that helps your partner feel heard.

- Focus your attention on your partner (turn toward your partner; ignore defensive thoughts).

- Try to understand both the thoughts and the feelings (you don't have to agree!).

- Show that you understand (paraphrase).

Appendix B

<u>Speak</u> in a way that makes it easier to listen.

- Give your partner the benefit of the doubt (you could be wrong; they're not stupid or evil).

- Lead with the positive (start with a positive comment rather than a complaint).

- Avoid blaming and name-calling (don't say things to make your partner defensive).

- Speak mostly about your own thoughts and feelings (talk about what's inside of you; when you say something about your partner, focus on behavior).

- Focus on the present (don't dredge up the past).

- Make room for your partner to respond (don't dump; pause frequently).

Appendix C

Responding to My Partner's Answers

(Note: you should have *six* copies of this handout, one for each section of the CJ.)

My name:_____ Topic:_____

In this section of the Conversation Jumpstarter, what I like about my partner's answer is . . .

What I have a question about is . . .

What worries or concerns me is . . .

Check one in each column:

How important is it to you
to discuss this topic?

How difficult do you think it will
be for you personally to discuss this topic?

❏ Very important
❏ Moderately important
❏ A little important
❏ Not important at all

❏ Very difficult
❏ Moderately difficult
❏ A little difficult
❏ Not difficult at all

Appendix D

Practice Communication Exercise

The point of this exercise is to practice your Constructive Communication skills, using the same structure you already did when you met with your coach. Choose one topic from the Conversation Jumpstarter (CJ) to discuss as a couple, and then engage in three "mini-conversations" based on what you wrote on the corresponding page from "Responding to My Partner's Answers."

Important: Be intentional about following the Constructive Communication guidelines every time you speak and listen. Remember in particular that when it's your turn to listen, your job is to show that you understand, even if you don't agree.

If at any point during the exercise you become upset, take a break, then come back and try again. If it's still difficult, turn your chairs so that you can hear but not see each other. If that still doesn't help, stop the exercise and wait to discuss it at the next session with your coach.

Make sure you have at least one hour of uninterrupted time for the exercise. Sit in comfortable chairs, facing each other. Choose one person to be the first speaker. Have three mini-conversations as follows:

- Mini-conversation 1: What did you like about your partner's answer?
  Talk about one thing you liked at a time. Using constructive communication, one of you takes the role of the speaker; the other listens. Take turns saying what you liked, but don't switch roles until the speaker feels heard and understood.

- Mini-conversation 2: What did you have a question about regarding your partner's answer?

This conversation has the same structure as the first one, with one addition: when the speaker agrees that the listener has understood the question, then the listener becomes the speaker and responds. Again, take turns stating your questions, and always follow the guidelines for both listening and speaking.

- Mini-conversation 3: What worried or concerned you about your partner's answer?
  This conversation is similar to the second one. When the speaker agrees that the listener has heard the concern well, the listener may become the speaker and respond. Take turns stating your concerns.

When the three mini-conversations are finished, debrief the experience together. Talk about how it felt to do the exercise, what you learned, and how you would like to apply what you learned to your relationship.

Appendix E

Making Our Marriage Stronger

My name: _____

Couples often complain that after the wedding and honeymoon are over, they stop courting each other and begin taking their relationship for granted. This exercise will help you keep your marriage strong by identifying the things you like most about your relationship now, and planning how you will maintain them for the future.

1.   Think about the positive things your partner does in your relationship. For example, what does he or she do to . . .

- show interest in your thoughts, feelings, and opinions?
- show that he or she cares and is thinking about you?
- express appreciation for what you do?
- express physical affection?
- express concern when you're feeling low?
- communicate that he or she accepts you for who you are?
- keep things fun or humorous?

In the space below, list the positive behaviors that are most important to you:

2.   Think of two stories that illustrate these or other similar positive things your partner has done for you. Use the space below to jot a few notes to yourself about the key points of each story:

• Notes for story 1

• Notes for story 2

3.   Now take turns telling each other your stories. Keep the conversation positive. Don't insert any criticisms or complaints; just tell stories about the things you like and would want to see more of in your relationship.

4.   When you've finished telling your stories, answer this question together: what positive things are you already doing for your relationship that you want to keep doing—or even do more of—after you're married? List at least two or three of them below:

5.   Now, make a plan. What, concretely, will you do to make sure these things stay in your relationship? Don't be vague; describe what you will do in enough detail that somebody else would be able to understand it and do it himself or herself. In the space below, write down at least two concrete behaviors to which you will commit to make your marriage stronger.

Making Decisions When Our Needs Conflict

This handout will walk you through a strategy for resolving conflict when there is a decision to be made and the two of you don't agree. Your coach will help you with the exercise.

1. *Define the specific disagreement to be discussed.*

What is the practical decision that needs to be made? Write it in the space below.

Wife, complete this sentence in the space below: "The solution I want is . . ."

Husband, complete this sentence in the space below: "The solution I want is . . ."

2. *Redefine the conflict in terms of needs.*

Wife, thinking about what you wrote above, complete this sentence in the space below: "I want that solution because I need to know or feel . . ."

Husband, thinking about what you wrote above, complete this sentence in the space below: "I want that solution because I need to know or feel . . ."

Talk about these needs with each other, using Constructive Communication. *Important: Don't proceed to the next stage until you both feel heard and understood.*

3. *Brainstorm possible alternatives.*

On a separate sheet of paper, take about ten to fifteen minutes to write down as many possible solutions as you can think of, regardless of how silly they might seem. You will have to give up, at least temporarily, your desire to lobby for your preferred solution. Be creative and have fun; at this stage, there are no bad or wrong answers.

4. *Agree on one alternative and make a plan.*

Now go back over your list and decide on one alternative to try. It should be one that you agree gives the best chance of meeting the needs you both expressed in step 2. Write down your choice here:

Make a plan. Discuss what concrete steps need to be taken. Jot notes to yourselves below so that it's clear who is responsible to do what and by when.

5. *Schedule a progress review.*

Think about how much time you need, reasonably, to give the solution a fair trial period. Then make a specific appointment with each other to come back and talk about how well the solution is working for both of you in terms of the needs discussed earlier. Write the date and time of your scheduled progress review below, and put it on your calendar:

Date: Time:

Notes

Introduction

1. David H. Olson, Amy Olson-Sigg, and Peter J. Larson, *The Couple Checkup* (Nashville: Thomas Nelson, 2008), 21.

2. See, for example, Scott M. Stanley, Galena K. Rhoades, and Howard J. Markman, "Sliding Versus Deciding: Inertia and the Premarital Cohabitation Effect," *Family Relations* 55 (2006): 499–509.

3. One recent article reports that in a survey of more than three thousand American adults, 44 percent of participants who married since 1990 had participated in some form of premarital education. See Scott M. Stanley et al., "Premarital Education, Marital Quality, and Marital Stability: Findings from a Large Random Household Survey," *Journal of Family Psychology* 20 (2006): 117–26.

4. For more information on the inventories and on training opportunities, visit their websites at www.prepare-enrich.com and www.foccusinc.com.

1. The Basic Skills

1. We'll say more about policy in the epilogue at the end of the book.

2. Here are some useful books that could be given to couples: David P. Gushee, *Getting Marriage Right* (Grand Rapids: Baker, 2004); Gary Thomas, *Sacred Marriage* (Grand Rapids: Zondervan, 2000). Gushee's book would be a somewhat more difficult read for many couples, but worth the effort; it would also make an excellent starting point for thinking theologically about a congregation's marriage ministry.

3. John M. Gottman, *The Marriage Clinic* (New York: W. W. Norton, 1999), 16.

4. This begs the question: *should* money be involved? Much depends on: (a) your level of training; (b) how you understand what you are doing; and (c) how you want the work to be perceived. Being paid session by session evokes expectations that are more related to professional psychotherapy services than pastoral ministry. That makes the most sense if you're trained to provide therapy services and are doing preparation work that is independent of wedding officiation. But if you are also officiating the wedding, you may want the preparation process to be understood more

in ministry terms, as a sign of your pastoral commitment to the importance of marriage. Our conservative recommendation is that unless you intend to present yourself as a professional counselor, then offer premarital preparation as one of your ministries and let the couple decide on their own what honorarium might be appropriate.

5. See principle 1.8, available at http://www.aamft.org/imis15/content/legal_ethics/code_of_ethics.aspx.

6. The registry can be found at http://marriagefriendlytherapists.com. You can search for therapists by state and zip code. The values statement can be found at http://marriagefriendlytherapists.com/values.php.

2. Dealing with Difference

1. Barbara D. Whitehead and David Popenoe, "Who Wants to Marry a Soul Mate?" 6, 7. The essay is part of the National Marriage Project's annual report for 2001, *The State of Our Unions 2001: The Social Health of Marriage in America.* The full report is available online at http://www.stateofourunions.org/pdfs/SOOU2001.pdf.

2. Blaine J. Fowers, *Beyond the Myth of Marital Happiness* (San Francisco: Jossey-Bass, 2000), 73.

3. Betsy Yphantides, in Jerusha Clark, *When I Get Married: Surrendering the Fantasy, Embracing the Reality* (Colorado Springs: NavPress, 2009), 27–28.

4. John Gray, *Men Are from Mars, Women Are from Venus,* paperback ed. (New York: HarperCollins, 2012). The success of the original has spawned a veritable cottage industry of Mars/Venus books, applying the ideas to male-female relationships in every setting from the bedroom to the boardroom.

5. Ibid., 9.

6. Ibid., 11.

7. Deborah Tannen, *You Just Don't Understand: Women and Men in Conversation* (New York: Ballantine, 1990), 42.

8. Emerson Eggerichs, *Love and Respect* (Nashville: Thomas Nelson, 2004); see also his more recent work, *Cracking the Communication Code* (Nashville: Thomas Nelson, 2007). It should be noted that Paul's word for "love" is *agapa*, which is commanded of all Christians, not just husbands; the word for "respect" is *phobe*, suggesting a reverent fear that is probably a bit more than what Eggerichs intends by respect.

9. Shaunti Feldhahn, *For Women Only: What You Need to Know about the Inner Lives of Men* (Colorado Springs: Multnomah, 2004), 21–22. Interestingly, John Gray lists respect as one of *women's* primary emotional needs rather than men's (*Men Are from Mars, Women Are from Venus,* 145).

10. For a well-argued and trenchant criticism of gender stereotypes and their implications, see Rosalind Barnett and Caryl Rivers, *Same Difference* (New York: Basic, 2004), especially their critique of John Gray on pp. 106–12.

11. Joel Crohn, *Mixed Matches* (New York: Fawcett Columbine, 1995), 74.

12. Ibid., 74–78.

13. Gray's description is reminiscent of John Gottman's notion of "stonewalling." See John M. Gottman, *The Marriage Clinic* (New York: W. W. Norton, 1999), 46–47. The difference is that Gray is close to normalizing what Gottman more clearly recognizes as part of destructive relationship pattern.

14. Gray, *Men Are from Mars, Women Are from Venus*, 30.

15. It's possible for the attribution error to work the other way around, such that the blame falls on your situation or my character.

16. Terry D. Hargrave, *The Essential Humility of Marriage: Honoring the Third Identity in Couple Therapy* (Phoenix: Zeig, Tucker & Theisen, 2000).

3. Using the *Conversation Jumpstarter*: A Flexible Four-Session Framework

1. Scott M. Stanley et al., "Premarital Education, Marital Quality, and Marital Stability: Findings from a Large Random Household Survey," *Journal of Family Psychology* 20 (2006): 117–26; Jason S. Carroll and William J. Doherty, "Evaluating the Effectiveness of Premarital Prevention Programs: A Meta-Analytic Review of Outcome Research," *Family Relations* 52 (2003): 105–18. For a more general resource, see Patty Howell's succinct 2011 monograph, *The Case for Relationship Education*, published by Healthy Relationships California, and available at http://www.relationshipsca.org/store/free-resources?page=2.

2. Elizabeth B. Fawcett et al., "Do Premarital Education Programs Really Work? A Meta-Analytic Study," *Family Relations* 59 (2010): 232–39.

4. Communication That Builds Relationship

1. Clifford Notarius and Howard J. Markman, *We Can Work It Out* (New York: Perigree, 1993), 22.

2. For a thorough and highly readable introduction to the stress response and its health implications, see Robert Sapolsky, *Why Zebras Don't Get Ulcers*, 3rd ed. (New York: Henry Holt, 2004).

3. John Gottman recommends taking a break when one's heart rate is 10 percent above baseline, and suggests that this is "absolutely crucial" if one's rate climbs above one hundred beats per minute. Check your pulse for fifteen seconds; if it's over twenty-five beats, take a break. See John Gottman and Nan Silver, *Why Marriages Succeed or Fail* (New York: Fireside, 1994), 177.

4. See Archibald D. Hart, *Adrenaline and Stress* (Dallas: Word, 1995), 118–22.

5. Gottman and Silver, *Why Marriages Succeed or Fail*, 178.

6. Ibid., 179.

7. The skill is called "Power Listening Lite." See Patty Howell and Ralph Jones, *World Class Marriage* (Lanham, MD: Rowman & Littlefield, 2010), 38–39.

8. The recommendations that follow are a hybrid of similar principles taught across a variety of curricula. Among the most widely known are Thomas Gordon's

"active listening" as described in *P.E.T.: Parent Effectiveness Training* (New York: New American Library, 1970), and the "Speaker-Listener Technique" of the PREP (Prevention and Relationship Enhancement Program) approach; for the latter, see Howard J. Markman, Scott M. Stanley, and Susan L. Blumberg, *Fighting for Your Marriage*, rev. ed. (San Francisco: Jossey-Bass, 2001). For a Christian version of the PREP program, see Scott Stanley et al., *A Lasting Promise* (San Francisco: Jossey-Bass, 1998). The most thorough treatment of the why and how of listening, however, is Michael Nichols's *The Lost Art of Listening*, 2nd ed. (New York: Guilford, 2009).

9. Virginia and Redford Williams, *Lifeskills* (New York: Times Books, 1997), 87.

10. John Gottman and Nan Silver, *The Seven Principles for Making Marriage Work* (New York: Three Rivers Press, 1999), 157–85.

11. The concept traces back to Thomas Gordon's *Parent Effectiveness Training* (New York: P. H. Wyden, 1970), an application of Carl Rogers's psychology to parent-child communication. Some version of the concept is taught in most relationship communication curricula.

5. Facing Conflict Together as a Couple

1. John Gottman and Nan Silver, *Why Marriages Succeed or Fail* (New York: Fireside, 1994), 56–61.

2. Ibid., 72. Gottman called these four conflict behaviors the "Four Horsemen of the Apocalypse," emphasizing the ways in which each behavior cascaded into the next, and through their combined effect left couples more likely to divorce.

3. Barbara Fredrickson, "The Role of Positive Emotions in Positive Psychology: The Broaden-and-Build Theory of Positive Emotions," *American Psychologist* 56 (2001): 218–26.

4. For example, see Gottman, *Why Marriages Succeed or Fail*, 59–61.

5. Susan M. Johnson calls this the "protest polka." See her book *Hold Me Tight* (New York: Little, Brown, 2008), 74–86.

6. See Thomas Gordon, *Parent Effectiveness Training* (New York: P. H. Wyden, 1970), chapter 11. According to Patty Howell and Ralph Jones, Gordon in turn adapted his method from John Dewey's six-step problem-solving procedure. See Howell and Jones, *World Class Marriage* (Lanham, MD: Rowman & Littlefield, 2010), 87.

7. See, for example, the "Problem Solution" technique of the PREP (Prevention and Relationship Enhancement Program) approach, in Howard J. Markman, Scott M. Stanley, and Susan L. Blumberg, *Fighting for Your Marriage*, rev. ed. (San Francisco: Jossey-Bass, 2001), as well as Andrew Christensen and Neil Jacobson, *Acceptance and Change in Couple Therapy* (New York: W. W. Norton, 1998), and their related work written for couples, *Reconcilable Differences* (New York: Guilford, 2000).

6. Coaching the Conversations

1. This is a variation of a skill taught by Family Wellness Associates when certifying instructors in their *Survival Skills for Healthy Families* curriculum. For more information on training, go to www.familywellness.com.

2. See John Gottman, *The Marriage Clinic* (New York: W.W. Norton, 1999), 124–25 for a more complete list.

3. Daniel M. Wegner, "How to Think, Say, or Do Precisely the Worst Thing for Any Occasion," *Science* 325 (2009): 48–50.

4. John Gottman and Nan Silver, *The Seven Principles for Making Marriage Work* (New York: Three Rivers Press, 1999), 22–23.

7. Roles and Responsibilities

1. Jessie Bernard first popularized the terms in *The Future of Marriage* (New York: World, 1972). More recently, Janice M. Steil, in her book *Marital Equality* (Thousand Oaks, CA: Sage, 1997), argues that Bernard's basic thesis is still correct, despite the growth in women's paid work. However, Linda Waite and Maggie Gallagher argue that current evidence points away from Bernard's conclusions; see *The Case for Marriage* (New York: Doubleday, 2000), chapter 12.

2. Arlie Hochschild and Anne Machung, *The Second Shift* (New York: Avon, 1989).

3. Willard Harley, *His Needs, Her Needs* (Grand Rapids: Revell, 2001), 135.

4. "Wives Still Do Laundry, Men Do Yard Work," April 4, 2008. Available online at http://www.gallup.com/poll/106249/wives-still-laundry-men-yard-work.aspx.

5. Michelle L. Frisco and Kristi Williams, "Perceived Housework Equity, Marital Happiness, and Divorce in Dual-Earner Households," *Journal of Family Issues* 24 (2003): 51–73.

6. See Matthijs Kalmijn and Christiaan W. S. Monden, "The Division of Labor and Depressive Symptoms at the Couple Level: Effects of Equity or Specialization?" *Journal of Social and Personal Relationships* 29 (2011): 358–74; Kathryn J. Lively, Lala Carr Steelman, and Brian Powell, "Equity, Emotion, and Household Division of Labor Response," *Social Psychology Quarterly* 73 (2010): 358–79.

7. Rosalind C. Barnett and Caryl Rivers distinguish between high- and low-control tasks, noting that traditionally male tasks tend to be the former, while traditionally female ones tend to be the latter. See their book *She Works, He Works* (Cambridge, MA: Harvard University Press, 1996), 179.

8. Bureau of Labor Statistics, "Changes in Men's and Women's Labor Force Participation Rates," 2007. Available online at http://www.bls.gov/opub/ted/2007/jan/wk2/art03.htm.

9. Liza Mundy writes: "Wives are breadwinners or co-earners in about two-thirds of American marriages. Among families with working wives, the percentage in which the wife outearns the husband has gone up dramatically, from 23.7 percent in 1987 to 37.7 percent in 2009. . . . Gains have been highest for more educated wives,

which means breadwinning women are no longer just the wives of poor men. . . . Almost 7 percent of wives . . . were sole breadwinners. The share of husbands who were the sole breadwinner declined from 35 percent in 1967 to 18 percent in 2009." See *The Richer Sex* (New York: Simon & Schuster, 2012), 39.

10. Barnett and Rivers, *She Works, He Works*, 192.

8. Love and Affection

1. Jack O. Balswick and Judith K. Balswick, *Authentic Human Sexuality: An Integrated Christian Approach*, 2nd ed. (Downers Grove, IL: InterVarsity Press, 2008).

2. Gary Chapman, *Toward a Growing Marriage: Building the Love Relationship of Your Dreams* (Chicago: Moody Press, 1996).

3. Barry McCarthy and Emily McCarthy, *Rekindling Desire* (New York: Brunner-Routledge, 2003).

4. Charles A. Wilkinson, "Expressing Affection: A Vocabulary of Loving Messages," in Kathleen M. Galvin and Pamela J. Cooper, eds., *Making Connections*, 4th ed. (Los Angeles: Roxbury, 1999): 155–63.

5. Balswick and Balswick, *Authentic Human Sexuality*.

6. Howard J. Markman, Scott M. Stanley, and Susan L. Blumberg, *Fighting for Your Marriage*, rev. ed. (San Francisco: Jossey-Bass, 2001), 40.

7. Michael E. Metz and Barry McCarthy, "The 'Good-Enough Sex' Model for Couple Sexual Satisfaction," *Sexual and Relationship Therapy* 22 (2007): 351–62.

8. Scott Stanley, David Trathen, and Savannah McCain, *A Lasting Promise* (San Francisco: Jossey-Bass, 1998).

9. Metz and McCarthy, "The 'Good-Enough Sex' Model."

10. See, for example, Les Parrott and Leslie Parrott, *Saving Your Marriage Before It Starts Workbook for Women*, expanded ed. (Grand Rapids: Zondervan, 2006). "Self-test" number seven addresses myths about sexuality.

11. Metz and McCarthy, "The 'Good-Enough Sex' Model."

12. Ibid.

9. The Meaning of Money

1. Melanie Powell and David Ansic, "Gender Differences in Risk Behaviour in Financial Decision-Making: An Experimental Analysis," *Journal of Economic Psychology* 18 (1997): 605–28; Richard Lynn, "Sex Differences in Competitiveness and the Valuation of Money in Twenty Countries," *Journal of Social Psychology* 133 (1993): 507–11; Natalie H. Jenkins et al., *You Paid How Much for That?* (San Francisco: Jossey-Bass, 2002), 116–17.

2. For example, see Jason Zweig, *Your Money and Your Brain* (New York: Simon & Schuster, 2007).

3. David H. Olson, Amy Olson-Sigg, and Peter J. Larson, *The Couple Checkup* (Nashville: Thomas Nelson, 2008), 79–80.

4. Lauren M. Papp, E. Mark Cummings, and Marcie C. Goeke-Morey, "For Richer, for Poorer: Money as a Topic of Marital Conflict in the Home," *Family Relations* 58 (2009): 91–103.

5. Jenkins et al., *You Paid How Much for That?* 26.

6. Ibid., chapter 4.

7. Deborah Knuckey, *Conscious Spending for Couples: Seven Skills for Financial Harmony* (New York: John Wiley, 2003), 37.

8. Ibid., 39.

9. Tim Chen, "American Household Credit Card Debt Statistics through 2012." Report available online at http://www.nerdwallet.com/blog/credit-card-data /average-credit-card-debt-household/.

10. Linda M. Skogrand et al., "The Effects of Debt on Newlyweds and Implications for Education," *Journal of Extension* 43, no. 3 (June 2005). Available online at http://www.joe.org/joe/2005june/rb7.php.

11. Jeffrey Dew, "Debt Change and Marital Satisfaction Change in Recently Married Couples," *Family Relations* 57 (2008): 60–71.

12. Simple DTI calculators can be found online, for example, at http://www .bankrate.com/calculators/mortgages/ratio-debt-calculator.aspx. Use gross income for the calculation; a decent DTI is below thirty-six.

13. Heather Mahar, "Why Are There So Few Prenuptial Agreements?" (2003). *Harvard Law School John M. Olin Center for Law, Economics and Business Discussion Paper Series.* Paper 436. Available online at http://lsr.nellco.org/harvard_olin/436.

14. Patty Howell and Ralph Jones, *World Class Marriage* (Lanham, MD: Rowman & Littlefield, 2010), 80.

10. The Possibilities of Parenthood

1. Quoted in David H. Olson, Amy Olson-Sigg, and Peter J. Larson, *The Couple Checkup* (Nashville: Thomas Nelson, 2008), 191.

2. Jean M. Twenge, W. Keith Campbell, and Craig A. Foster, "Parenthood and Marital Satisfaction: A Meta-Analytic Review," *Journal of Marriage and Family* 65 (2003): 574–83. The meta-analysis included a total of more than forty-seven thousand respondents. More childless couples rate themselves as highly satisfied in their marriages than do parents: 55 percent versus 45 percent, respectively. Between childless women and women with infants the contrast is more striking: 62 percent versus 38 percent.

3. Danielle M. Mitnick, Richard E. Heyman, and Amy M. Smith Slep, "Changes in Relationship Satisfaction across the Transition to Parenthood: A Meta-Analysis," *Journal of Family Psychology* 23 (2009): 848–52.

4. Renske Keizer and Niels Schenk, "Becoming a Parent and Relationship Satisfaction: A Longitudinal Dyadic Perspective," *Journal of Marriage and Family* 74 (2012): 759–73.

5. Esther S. Kluwer and Matthew D. Johnson, "Conflict Frequency and Relationship Quality Across the Transition to Parenthood," *Journal of Marriage and the Family* 69 (2007): 1089–106.

6. Twenge et al., "Parenthood and Marital Satisfaction," 582.

7. E. Mavis Hetherington and John Kelly, *For Better or Worse: Divorce Reconsidered* (New York: W. W. Norton, 2002), 181.

8. Ellen Galinsky, *The Six Stages of Parenthood* (Reading, MA: Perseus, 1987), 16–17.

9. See Diana Baumrind, "Effects of Authoritative Parental Control on Child Behavior," *Child Development* 37 (1966): 887–907; "Child Care Practices Anteceding Three Patterns of Preschool Behavior," *Genetic Psychology Monographs* 75 (1967): 43–88.

10. See, for example, Leon Kuczynski, Susan Lollis, and Yuiko Koguchi, "Reconstructing Common Sense: Metaphors of Bidirectionality in Parent-Child Relations," in *Handbook of Dynamics in Parent-Child Relations*, ed. Leon Kuczynski (Thousand Oaks, CA: Sage, 2003), 421–37.

11. See, for example, Diana Baumrind, Robert E. Larzelere, and Elizabeth B. Owens, "Effects of Preschool Parents' Power Assertive Patterns and Practices on Adolescent Development," *Parenting: Science and Practice* 10 (2010): 157–201, which concludes that how parents treat their children in preschool shapes their adjustment in adolescence.

12. See, for example, Nadia Sorkhabi, "Applicability of Baumrind's Parent Typology to Collective Cultures: Analysis of Cultural Explanations of Parent Socialization Effects," *International Journal of Behavioral Development* 29 (2005): 552–63; Brian K. Barber, Heidi E. Stoltz, and Joseph A. Olsen, "Parental Support, Psychological Control, and Behavioral Control: Assessing Relevance across Time, Culture, and Method: VIII. Discussion," *Monographs of the Society for Research in Child Development* 70 (2005): 105–24.

13. Ron L. Deal and David H. Olson, *The Remarriage Checkup* (Bloomington, MN: Bethany House, 2010), 104.

14. Hetherington and Kelly, *For Better or Worse*, 201.

15. Kay Pasley, David C. Dollahite, and Marilyn Ihinger-Tallman, "Bridging the Gap: Clinical Application of Research Findings on the Spouse and Stepparent Roles in Remarriage," *Family Relations* 42 (1993): 318.

16. Emily B. Visher and John S. Visher, *Therapy with Stepfamilies* (New York: Brunner/Mazel, 1996).

11. In-Laws and Extended Family

1. Evelyn Duvall, *In-Laws, Pro and Con* (New York: Association Press, 1954).

2. Susan G. Timmer and Joseph Veroff, "Family Ties and the Discontinuity of Divorce in Black and White Newlywed Couples," *Journal of Marriage and Family* 62 (2000): 349–61.

3. Chalandra M. Bryant, Rand D. Conger, and Jennifer M. Meehan, "The Influence of In-Laws on Change in Marital Success," *Journal of Marriage and Family* 63 (2001): 614–26.

4. Judith L. Silverstein, "The Problem with In-Laws," *Journal of Family Therapy* 14 (1992): 399–412.

5. Jack O. Balswick and Judith K. Balswick, *A Model for Marriage* (Downers Grove, IL: InterVarsity Press, 2006).

6. Gary Chapman, *Toward a Growing Marriage* (Chicago: Moody Press, 1979). Biblical examples include the stories of Moses and Jethro, and Naomi and Ruth.

7. Terry D. Hargrave, *The Essential Humility of Marriage: Honoring the Third Identity in Couple Therapy* (Phoenix: Zeig, Tucker & Theisen, 2000).

8. Balswick and Balswick, *A Model for Marriage.*

9. Hargrave, *The Essential Humility of Marriage.*

12. Religious Devotion and Practice

1. The saying is attributed to Father Patrick Peyton, CSC, a twentieth-century Roman Catholic priest. See http://www.fatherpeyton.org.

2. Loren Marks, "Sacred Practices in Highly Religious Families: Christian, Jewish, Mormon, and Muslim Perspectives," *Family Process* 43 (2004): 217–31.

3. This similarity is known as "religious homogamy." See, for example, Scott M. Myers, "Religious Homogamy and Marital Quality: Historical and Generational Patterns, 1980–1997," *Journal of Marriage and Family* 68 (2006): 292–304. Myers argues that the positive influence of homogamy has waned over time as other cultural values have become more important.

4. See, for example, Jo Berry, *Beloved Unbeliever* (Grand Rapids: Zondervan, 1981); Lynn Donovan and Dineen Miller, *Winning Him without Words* (Ventura, CA: Regal, 2010); Nancy Kennedy, *When He Doesn't Believe* (Colorado Springs: WaterBrook Press, 2001); Lee Strobel and Leslie Strobel, *Surviving a Spiritual Mismatch in Marriage* (Grand Rapids: Zondervan, 2002).

5. In a similar vein, Nancy Kennedy wisely cautions spiritually lonely women to "guard their hearts," that is, not to form emotional attachments to Christian men by confiding their marital woes to them. See *When He Doesn't Believe*, 38.

6. Strobel and Strobel, *Surviving a Spiritual Mismatch.*

7. Nancy Kennedy writes from the perspective of a wife who became a Christian early in her marriage; after more than twenty years, her husband still had not given his life to Christ. She rightly observes that a wife in that situation should not put her hope in the saving effect of her good example, but should learn to trust in God's sovereignty instead. *When He Doesn't Believe*, 43.

8. Gary Chapman, *Things I Wish I'd Known Before We Got Married* (Chicago: Northfield Publishing, 2010), 115–16.

9. Strobel and Strobel, *Surviving a Spiritual Mismatch*, 154–55.

10. Billy Sunday, in *Billy Sunday: The Man and His Message with His Own Words Which Have Won Thousands for Christ*, ed. William T. Ellis (n.p.: L. T. Myers, 1914), 77. The language of the original has been altered to be gender inclusive.

11. Annette Mahoney et al., "Marriage and the Spiritual Realm: The Role of Proximal and Distal Religious Constructs in Marital Functioning," *Journal of Family Psychology* 13 (1999): 321–38; Margaret L. Vaaler, Christopher G. Ellison, and Daniel A. Powers, "Religious Influences on the Risk of Marital Dissolution," *Journal of Marriage and Family* 71 (2009): 917–34.

12. David C. Atkins and Deborah E. Kessel, "Religiousness and Infidelity: Attendance, but Not Faith and Prayer, Predict Marital Fidelity," *Journal of Marriage and Family* 70 (2004): 407–18.

13. Donovan and Miller, *Winning Him without Words*, 167–68.

Epilogue: The Big Picture

1. What we are describing is what Mike and Harriet McManus, founders of the nonprofit organization Marriage Savers, have called "community marriage policies," or CMPs. The McManuses claim that communities that adopt CMPs soon see a reduction in their divorce rate. Visit www.marriagesavers.org for more information on their research and on training opportunities.

Bibliography

American Association for Marriage and Family Therapy. "Code of Ethics." AAMFT .org. Last modified July 1, 2012. http://www.aamft.org/imis15/content/legal_ethics/code_of_ethics.aspx.

Arp, David, Claudia Arp, Curt Brown, and Natelle Brown. *10 Great Dates Before You Say "I Do."* Grand Rapids: Zondervan, 2003.

Atkins, David C., and Deborah E. Kessel. "Religiousness and Infidelity: Attendance, but Not Faith and Prayer, Predict Marital Fidelity." *Journal of Marriage and Family* 70 (2004): 407–18.

Balswick, Jack O., and Judith K. Balswick. *A Model for Marriage.* Downers Grove, IL: InterVarsity Press, 2006.

———. *Authentic Human Sexuality: An Integrated Christian Approach.* 2nd ed. Downers Grove, IL: InterVarsity Press, 2008.

Barber, Brian K., Heidi E. Stoltz, and Joseph A. Olsen. "Parental Support, Psychological Control, and Behavioral Control: Assessing Relevance across Time, Culture, and Method: VIII. Discussion." *Monographs of the Society for Research in Child Development* 70 (2005): 105–24.

Barnett, Rosalind C., and Caryl Rivers. *Same Difference.* New York: Basic, 2004.

———. *She Works, He Works.* Cambridge, MA: Harvard University Press, 1996.

Baumrind, Diana. "Child Care Practices Anteceding Three Patterns of Preschool Behavior." *Genetic Psychology Monographs* 75 (1967): 43–88.

———. "Effects of Authoritative Parental Control on Child Behavior." *Child Development* 37 (1966): 887–907.

Baumrind, Diana, Robert E. Larzelere, and Elizabeth B. Owens. "Effects of Preschool Parents' Power Assertive Patterns and Practices on Adolescent Development." *Parenting: Science and Practice* 10 (2010): 157–201.

Bernard, Jessie. *The Future of Marriage.* New York: World, 1972.

Berry, Jo. *Beloved Unbeliever.* Grand Rapids: Zondervan, 1981.

Bryant, Chalandra M., Rand D. Conger, and Jennifer M. Meehan. "The Influence of In-Laws on Change in Marital Success." *Journal of Marriage and Family* 63 (2001): 614–26.

Bureau of Labor Statistics. "Changes in Men's and Women's Labor Force Participation Rates." 2007. Online: http://www.bls.gov/opub/ted/2007/jan/wk2/art03.htm.

Carroll, Jason S., and William J. Doherty. "Evaluating the Effectiveness of Premarital Prevention Programs: A Meta-Analytic Review of Outcome Research." *Family Relations* 52 (2003): 105–18.

Chapman, Gary. *Things I Wish I'd Known Before We Got Married.* Chicago: Northfield Publishing, 2010.

———. *Toward a Growing Marriage: Building the Relationship of Your Dreams.* Chicago: Moody Press, 1996.

Chen, Tim. "American Household Credit Card Debt Statistics through 2012." Online: http://www.nerdwallet.com/blog/credit-card-data/average-credit-card-debt-household/.

Christensen, Andrew, and Neil Jacobson. *Acceptance and Change in Couple Therapy.* New York: W. W. Norton, 1998.

———. *Reconcilable Differences.* New York: Guilford Press, 2000.

Clark, Jerusha. *When I Get Married: Surrendering the Fantasy, Embracing the Reality.* Colorado Springs: NavPress, 2009.

Crohn, Joel. *Mixed Matches.* New York: Fawcett Columbine, 1995.

Deal, Ron L., and David H. Olson. *The Remarriage Checkup.* Bloomington, MN: Bethany House, 2010.

Dew, Jeffrey. "Debt Change and Marital Satisfaction Change in Recently Married Couples." *Family Relations* 57 (2008): 60–71.

Donovan, Lynn, and Dineen Miller. *Winning Him without Words.* Ventura, CA: Regal, 2010.

Duvall, Evelyn. *In-Laws, Pro and Con.* New York: Association Press, 1954.

Eggerichs, Emerson. *Cracking the Communication Code.* Nashville: Thomas Nelson, 2007.

———. *Love and Respect.* Nashville: Thomas Nelson, 2004.

Fawcett, Elizabeth B., Alan J. Hawkins, Victoria L. Blanchard, and Jason S. Carroll. "Do Premarital Education Programs Really Work? A Meta-Analytic Study." *Family Relations* 59 (2010): 232–39.

Feldhahn, Shaunti. *For Women Only: What You Need to Know about the Inner Lives of Men.* Colorado Springs: Multnomah, 2004.

Forward, Susan. *Toxic In-Laws.* New York: HarperCollins, 2001.

Fowers, Blaine J. *Beyond the Myth of Marital Happiness.* San Francisco: Jossey-Bass, 2000.

Fredrickson, Barbara. "The Role of Positive Emotions in Positive Psychology: The Broaden-and-Build Theory of Positive Emotions." *American Psychologist* 56 (2001): 218–26.

Frisco, Michelle L., and Kristi Williams. "Perceived Housework Equity, Marital Happiness, and Divorce in Dual-Earner Households." *Journal of Family Issues* 24 (2003): 51–73.

Galinsky, Ellen. *The Six Stages of Parenthood.* Reading, MA: Perseus, 1987.

Gordon, Thomas. *Parent Effectiveness Training.* New York: P. H. Wyden, 1970.

Gottman, John. *The Marriage Clinic.* New York: W. W. Norton, 1999.

Gottman, John, and Nan Silver. *The Seven Principles for Making Marriage Work*. New York: Three Rivers Press, 1999.

———. *Why Marriages Succeed or Fail*. New York: Fireside, 1994.

Gray, John. *Men Are from Mars, Women Are from Venus*. New York: HarperCollins, 1992.

Gushee, David P. *Getting Marriage Right*. Grand Rapids: Baker, 2004.

Hargrave, Terry D. *The Essential Humility of Marriage: Honoring the Third Identity in Couple Therapy*. Phoenix: Zeig, Tucker & Theisen, 2000.

Harley, Willard. *His Needs, Her Needs*. Grand Rapids: Revell, 2001.

Hart, Archibald D. *Adrenaline and Stress*. Dallas: Word, 1995.

Hetherington, E. Mavis, and John Kelly. *For Better or Worse: Divorce Reconsidered*. New York: W. W. Norton, 2002.

Hochschild, Arlie, and Anne Machung. *The Second Shift*. New York: Avon, 1989.

Howell, Patty. *The Case for Relationship Education*. N.p.: Healthy Relationships California, 2011.

Howell, Patty, and Ralph Jones. *World Class Marriage*. Lanham, MD: Rowman & Littlefield, 2010.

Jenkins, Natalie H., Scott M. Stanley, William C. Bailey, and Howard J. Markman. *You Paid How Much for That?* San Francisco: Jossey-Bass, 2002.

Johnson, Susan M. *Hold Me Tight*. New York: Little, Brown, 2008.

Jordan, Pamela L., Scott M. Stanley, and Howard J. Markman. *Becoming Parents: How to Strengthen Your Marriage as Your Family Grows*. San Francisco: Jossey-Bass, 1999.

Kalmijn, Matthijs, and Christiaan W. S. Monden. "The Division of Labor and Depressive Symptoms at the Couple Level: Effects of Equity or Specialization?" *Journal of Social and Personal Relationships* 29 (2011): 358–74.

Keizer, Renske, and Niels Schenk. "Becoming a Parent and Relationship Satisfaction: A Longitudinal Dyadic Perspective." *Journal of Marriage and Family* 74 (2012): 759–73.

Kennedy, Nancy. *When He Doesn't Believe*. Colorado Springs: WaterBrook Press, 2001.

Kluwer, Esther S., and Matthew D. Johnson. "Conflict Frequency and Relationship Quality across the Transition to Parenthood." *Journal of Marriage and the Family* 69 (2007): 1089–106.

Knuckey, Deborah. *Conscious Spending for Couples: Seven Skills for Financial Harmony*. New York: John Wiley, 2003.

Kuczynski, Leon, Susan Lollis, and Yuiko Koguchi. "Reconstructing Common Sense: Metaphors of Bidirectionality in Parent-Child Relations." In *Handbook of Dynamics in Parent-Child Relations*, edited by Leon Kuczynski, 421–37. Thousand Oaks, CA: Sage, 2003.

Lively, Kathryn J., Lala Carr Steelman, and Brian Powell. "Equity, Emotion, and Household Division of Labor Response." *Social Psychology Quarterly* 73 (2010): 358–79.

Lynn, Richard. "Sex Differences in Competitiveness and the Valuation of Money in Twenty Countries." *Journal of Social Psychology* 133 (1993): 507–11.

Mahar, Heather. "Why Are There So Few Prenuptial Agreements?" (2003). *Harvard Law School John M. Olin Center for Law, Economics and Business Discussion Paper Series.* Paper 436. Online: http://lsr.nellco.org/harvard_olin/436.

Mahoney, Annette, Kenneth I. Pargament, Tracey Jewell, Aaron B. Swank, Eric Scott, Erin Emery, and Mark Rye. "Marriage and the Spiritual Realm: The Role of Proximal and Distal Religious Constructs in Marital Functioning." *Journal of Family Psychology* 13 (1999): 321–38.

Markman, Howard J., Scott M. Stanley, and Susan L. Blumberg. *Fighting for Your Marriage.* Rev. ed. San Francisco: Jossey-Bass, 2001.

Marks, Loren. "Sacred Practices in Highly Religious Families: Christian, Jewish, Mormon, and Muslim Perspectives." *Family Process* 43 (2004): 217–31.

McCarthy, Barry, and Emily McCarthy. *Rekindling Desire.* New York: Brunner-Routledge, 2003.

Metz, Michael E., and Barry McCarthy. "The 'Good-Enough Sex' Model for Couple Sexual Satisfaction." *Sexual and Relationship Therapy* 22 (2007): 351–62.

Mitnick, Danielle M., Richard E. Heyman, and Amy M. Smith Slep. "Changes in Relationship Satisfaction across the Transition to Parenthood: A Meta-Analysis." *Journal of Family Psychology* 23 (2009): 848–52.

Mundy, Liza. *The Richer Sex.* New York: Simon & Schuster, 2012.

Myers, Scott M. "Religious Homogamy and Marital Quality: Historical and Generational Patterns, 1980–1997." *Journal of Marriage and Family* 68 (2006): 292–304.

The National Registry of Marriage Friendly Therapists. "Marriage Friendly Therapists." Last modified 2013. http://www.marriagefriendlytherapists.com.

Nichols, Michael. *The Lost Art of Listening.* 2nd ed. New York: Guilford Press, 2009.

Notarius, Clifford, and Howard Markman. *We Can Work It Out.* New York: Perigree, 1993.

Olson, David H., Amy Olson-Sigg, and Peter J. Larson. *The Couple Checkup.* Nashville: Thomas Nelson, 2008.

Papp, Lauren M., E. Mark Cummings, and Marcie C. Goeke-Morey. "For Richer, for Poorer: Money as a Topic of Marital Conflict in the Home." *Family Relations* 58 (2009): 91–103.

Parrott, Les, and Leslie Parrott. *Saving Your Marriage Before It Starts Workbook for Women.* Expanded ed. Grand Rapids: Zondervan, 2006.

Pasley, Kay, David C. Dollahite, and Marilyn Ihinger-Tallman. "Bridging the Gap: Clinical Application of Research Findings on the Spouse and Stepparent Roles in Remarriage." *Family Relations* 42 (1993): 315–22.

Penner, Clifford L., and Joyce J. Penner. *Getting Your Sex Life Off to a Great Start: A Guide for Engaged and Newlywed Couples.* Nashville: Thomas Nelson, 1994.

———. *The Gift of Sex.* Nashville: W Publishing Group, 2003.

Peyton, Patrick. "Father Patrick Peyton CSC." Holy Cross Family Ministries. Accessed July 12, 2013. http://www.fatherpeyton.org.

Powell, Melanie, and David Ansic. "Gender Differences in Risk Behaviour in Financial Decision-Making: An Experimental Analysis." *Journal of Economic Psychology* 18 (1997): 605–28.

Sapolsky, Robert. *Why Zebras Don't Get Ulcers.* 3rd ed. New York: Henry Holt, 2004.

Silverstein, Judith L. "The Problem with In-Laws." *Journal of Family Therapy* 14 (1992): 399–412.

Skogrand, Linda M., David G. Schramm, James P. Marshall, and Thomas R. Lee. "The Effects of Debt on Newlyweds and Implications for Education." *Journal of Extension* 43 (June 2005). Online: http://www.joe.org/joe/2005june/rb7.php.

Sorkhabi, Nadia. "Applicability of Baumrind's Parent Typology to Collective Cultures: Analysis of Cultural Explanations of Parent Socialization Effects." *International Journal of Behavioral Development* 29 (2005): 552–63.

Stanley, Scott M., Paul R. Amato, Christine A. Johnson, and Howard J. Markman. "Premarital Education, Marital Quality, and Marital Stability: Findings from a Large Random Household Survey." *Journal of Family Psychology* 20 (2006): 117–26.

Stanley, Scott M., Galena K. Rhoades, and Howard J. Markman. "Sliding Versus Deciding: Inertia and the Premarital Cohabitation Effect." *Family Relations* 55 (2006): 499–509.

Stanley, Scott, Daniel Trathen, Savanna McCain, and Milt Bryan. *A Lasting Promise.* San Francisco: Jossey-Bass, 1998.

Steil, Janice M. *Marital Equality.* Thousand Oaks, CA: Sage, 1997.

Strobel, Lee, and Leslie Strobel. *Surviving a Spiritual Mismatch in Marriage.* Grand Rapids: Zondervan, 2002.

Sunday, Billy. *Billy Sunday: The Man and His Message with His Own Words Which Have Won Thousands for Christ.* Edited by William T. Ellis. N.p.: L. T. Myers, 1914.

Tannen, Deborah. *You Just Don't Understand: Women and Men in Conversation.* New York: Ballantine, 1990.

Thomas, Gary. *Sacred Marriage.* Grand Rapids: Zondervan, 2000.

Timmer, Susan G., and Joseph Veroff. "Family Ties and the Discontinuity of Divorce in Black and White Newlywed Couples." *Journal of Marriage and Family* 62 (2000): 349–61.

Twenge, Jean M., W. Keith Campbell, and Craig A. Foster. "Parenthood and Marital Satisfaction: A Meta-Analytic Review." *Journal of Marriage and Family* 65 (2003): 574–83.

Vaaler, Margaret L., Christopher G. Ellison, and Daniel A. Powers. "Religious Influences on the Risk of Marital Dissolution." *Journal of Marriage and Family* 71 (2009): 917–34.

Visher, Emily B., and John S. Visher. *Therapy with Stepfamilies.* New York: Brunner/Mazel, 1996.

Waite, Linda, and Maggie Gallagher. *The Case for Marriage.* New York: Doubleday, 2000.

Wegner, Daniel M. "How to Think, Say, or Do Precisely the Worst Thing for Any Occasion." *Science* 325 (2009): 48–50.

Whitehead, Barbara D., and David Popenoe. "Who Wants to Marry a Soul Mate?" *The State of Our Unions 2001.* Online: http://www.stateofourunions.org/pdfs/SOOU2001.pdf.

Wilkinson, Charles A. "Expressing Affection: A Vocabulary of Loving Messages." In *Making Connections,* 4th ed., edited by Kathleen M. Galvin and Pamela J. Cooper, 155–63. Los Angeles: Roxbury, 1999.

Williams, Virginia, and Redford Williams. *Lifeskills.* New York: Times Books, 1997.

Zweig, Jason. *Your Money and Your Brain.* New York: Simon & Schuster, 2007.

Book Website Information

A message to our readers:

Thank you for purchasing and reading *Preparing Couples for Love and Marriage*. It is our fond and sincere hope that this book will lend valuable support to your premarital ministry.

To assist you further, we've created a website to accompany this book, http://preparing couples.com. There you can download printable copies of all the appendices for your own use with couples, read further tips from us, and share ideas from your own use of the Conversation Jumpstarter and the other tools. We'd love to hear from you.

May God bless couples through your faithful ministry!

—Cameron and Jim